From Sign to Symbol

Psychodynamic Psychotherapy and Assessment in the Twenty-First Century

Series Editors

Steven Tuber, City University of New York at City College

Mission Statement

Psychodynamic Psychotherapy and Assessment establishes a milieu for the presentation of scholarly clinical work through a developmental lens. The emphasis throughout the series is on the integration of scholarship and practice through writings that are informed by both sources of learning. This domain includes works that document both evidence-based and traditional approaches within the field and applies these approaches to work with infants, children, adolescents, and adults. Efforts that link assessment to treatment are especially welcome, as are integrations between neuropsychological (brain-based) and psychological (mind or self-based) formulations about personality development and its aberrations. The impact of trauma, both chronic and acute, on the psychological lives of its victims is also an important area of study within this domain. New voices within the field are encouraged to write about the interface between the content and process of their emergent thinking and practice. In addition to the areas mentioned above, more experienced clinical scholars are encouraged to write about the supervisory process and its impact on both theory and practice. Works that focus on specific developmental processes and paradigms at points throughout the lifespan are another welcome area for contributions.

Titles in the Series

Guided Enactments in Psychoanalytic Psychotherapy: A New Look at Therapy with Adults and Children, by Sebastiano Santostefano

From Sign to Symbol: Transformational Processes in Psychoanalysis, Psychotherapy, and Psychology, by Joseph Newirth

From Sign to Symbol

Transformational Processes in Psychoanalysis, Psychotherapy, and Psychology

Joseph Newirth

LEXINGTON BOOKS
Lanham • Boulder • New York • London

Published by Lexington Books
An imprint of The Rowman & Littlefield Publishing Group, Inc.
4501 Forbes Boulevard, Suite 200, Lanham, Maryland 20706
www.rowman.com

Unit A, Whitacre Mews, 26-34 Stannary Street, London SE11 4AB

British Library Cataloguing in Publication Information Available

Library of Congress Cataloging-in-Publication Data

Names: Newirth, Joseph, author.
Title: From sign to symbol : transformational processes in psychoanalysis, psychotherapy, and psychology / Joseph Newirth.
Description: Lanham : Lexington Books, [2017] | Series: Psychodynamic psychotherapy and assessment in the twenty-first century | Includes bibliographical references and index.
Identifiers: LCCN 2017060522 (print) | LCCN 2017059620 (ebook) | ISBN 9781498576857 (Electronic) | ISBN 9781498576840 (cloth : alk. paper)
Subjects: LCSH: Psychoanalysis. | Psychotherapy. | Psychology.
Classification: LCC RC506 (print) | LCC RC506 .N4953 2017 (ebook) | DDC 616.89/17--dc23
LC record available at https://lccn.loc.gov/2017060522

∞™ The paper used in this publication meets the minimum requirements of American National Standard for Information Sciences Permanence of Paper for Printed Library Materials, ANSI/NISO Z39.48-1992.

Printed in the United States of America

I want to dedicate this book to my family: Eleanor, Michael, Karen, Tyler, Hazel, and Violet. There are no words to express how much your love, kindness, humor, and encouragement have meant during this long journey. The most important part of any journey is returning home and I am so grateful that you are always there.

Contents

Acknowledgments

For the past decades I have had the good fortune of being a professor at the Gordon Derner School of Psychology at Adelphi University. I want to thank the university administration for supporting the work contained in this book and encouraging my inquiry into the dynamics of psychotherapy and psychoanalysis. My professional focus as an analyst, teacher, and supervisor has been on understanding how theory facilitates our understanding and improves our efforts in doing psychoanalysis and psychotherapy. This book also stands at a crossroads attempting to integrate the work of contemporary psychoanalysis and the academic disciplines of developmental, cognitive, and neuropsychology. The title, *From Sign to Symbol*, is meant to highlight the processes through which meaning is created and understood in modern psychoanalysis, psychotherapy, and psychology.

I owe an inordinate debt to my patients, supervisees, and students with whom I have been able to develop my understanding of the unconscious processes of symbolization in psychotherapy. I often feel that they are my co-authors. I am particularly grateful to Kristin Reale (2010) and Meredith Darcy (2010) for their generosity, courage, and openness in allowing me to present their clinical work in chapter 7. I also want to thank those colleagues who have closely worked with me including: Joyce Selter, Nirav Soni, Stephanie Lewin, Heidi Kling, Paul Steinberg, and Dana Tautfest. I also want to thank my graduate assistants who have helped bring this project to fruition: Sara Richardson, Alvaro Moreira, and John Burke.

It is hard for me to imagine having the fortitude to write without thanking the many colleagues and friends who have provided support and expressed enthusiasm for the ideas that have been developed in this book. I want to especially thank Steve Tuber, Kasey Beduhn, and Becca Rohde who have provided editorial support and encouragement throughout this project. I could not have done it without all of the support and assistance that I have received over the last two years.

Introduction

Lost in the Fog

Many years ago when I was sailing in a very thick fog, I heard two sailors talking on the radio. One was trying to help the other and asked, "where were you the last time you knew where you were?" This is a profound question. As psychoanalysts, psychotherapists, and psychologists, we know what it is like to be lost in fog, without a map or a compass which could provide coordinates for the analytic relationship and allow us to answer this persistent question: "where were you the last time you knew where you were?" I think of psychoanalytic theories like a series of nautical charts; intersecting maps, describing how the mind works and how the intersubjective fields of psychoanalysis and psychotherapy are organized. Like maps, different psychoanalytic theories were created at different times, have different purposes, and reflect movement in different time frames. Some maps focus on developmental theory, others on particular psychodynamic narratives, and still others on the moment to moment experience of analyst and patient in a therapy session. Our choice of maps are purposeful, personal, political, and aesthetic. My preferred maps integrate interpersonal, relational, Kleinian, and Lacanian theories and focus on the intersubjective development of the capacity for symbolic thought and mentalization in both conscious and unconscious realms. In this book I integrate contemporary intersubjective psychoanalytic theories with parallel developments in developmental, cognitive, and neuropsychological theories, which suggest a paradigm shift in contemporary approaches in the human sciences.

Freud's description of psychoanalysis as the "talking cure" firmly anchored it in the world of language, of signs and symbols. His revolutionary case studies described conversations through which his patients moved beyond their experiences of distress, often presented as concrete non-verbal experiences, actions, and behaviors outside of their control. These symptoms were understood as signs that pointed to more complex symbolic narratives of forgotten childhood experiences and intolerable wishes. From the beginning, psychoanalysis involved a transformation of signs into symbols, narratives which gave meaning to the mysteries of unwanted action. While this focus on symbolic transformation has been its core, the nature of this symbolic transformation has evolved from Freud's positivist perspective which focused on hidden truths, to the pragmatic, experiential perspectives of interpersonal and relational psychoanalysis which focused on purpose, to the postmodern, constructivist perspectives of object relations and Lacanian theory which focused on multiple meanings. These three perspectives represent different periods in the scientific and cultural zeitgeist of psychoanalysis, different approaches to the practice of psychotherapy and supervision, and different ways of conceptualizing the transformation of concrete experiences of signs and symptoms into symbolic experiences and narratives.

The classical one person, positivist paradigm structured psychotherapy as a search for hidden meanings, which Freud described using an archeological metaphor. The pragmatic, experiential, and constructivist paradigms of the twentieth century shifted this concept of transformation from the discovery of hidden truths to the expansion of experience and the construction of meaning; from a focus on the past to a focus on intersubjective experiences in the present, the development of future goals, intentions, and poetic or dream-like metaphors. Relational psychoanalysis focused on the importance of the patient's and analyst's mutual experience in the immediacy of the intersubjective transference countertransference relationship as providing new experiences which potentially expand both the analyst's and patient's relational patterns. Contemporary Kleinians also emphasize the intersubjective relationship between patient and analyst but conceived of this as providing a field for developing the internal structures through which symbolization can be developed.

Kleinian theory has consistently focused on the structures that underlie the capacity for symbolization, which was initially described as the concrete thinking of the paranoid schizoid position in which the word and the object were experienced as the same thing, in contrast to the complex integrated symbols of the depressive position in which the word represented but was not identical with the object. In this book I will trace the evolution of the Kleinian theory of symbolization from Klein's first generation theories of the paranoid schizoid and depressive positions to the second generation of object relations theorists especially Bion's and Winnicott's parallel concepts of the container-contained and transitional experience which emphasized the importance of the intersubjective relationship in the development of the capacity for symbolic thought. The third generation of object relations theorists, including Matte-Blanco, Grotstein, Ogden, and Ferro, separated the dream-like symbolic experiences in subjective relationships from the rational symbols used in describing the objective world. These theorists have focused on the intersubjective processes of reverie in clinical work in whose critical element is creating the capacity for symbolic experiences through a mutual dream-like process of reverie. I trace the evolution of concepts of symbolization, alpha function, reverie, the container contained, and the use of transitional experiences within contemporary object relations theories and integrate these concepts within the relational paradigm emphasizing the transformation of concrete experiences and enactments within the transference countertransference relationship into metaphorical symbolic experiences.

This evolution in psychoanalytic theory has been echoed in other areas of psychology which have also evolved from static one person, positivist approaches focused on finding causes or meanings for behavior in the past, to intersubjective experiential, constructivist approaches emphasizing the importance of attachment relationships and the development of the capacity to generate meanings within intersubjective relationships. In developmental, cognitive, and neuropsychological theories, psychological growth and development are conceptualized as occurring within intersubjective relationships between parent and child, individuals and their social milieu, and the brain and the human environment. As in contemporary psychoanalysis, concepts of symbolization or mentalization have emerged as core concepts in developmental, cognitive, and neuropsychological theories. I believe that this converging conceptual development represent a paradigm shift in the human sciences which offer us an opportunity to bring psychoanalysis, psychotherapy, developmental, cognitive, and neuropsychology into a mutually influencing, beneficial dialogue of the human sciences.

In the clinical sections of this book I focus on the transformation of signs into symbols in psychoanalysis, psychotherapy, and psychoanalytic supervision. These examples focus on the development of the capacity for symbolization in patients, therapists, and supervisors. These clinical examples illustrate the process of transforming concrete experiences into symbolic experience; how we move from being reactive to the push and pull of inner and outer stimuli, to being self-reflective, thoughtful, and able to understand another's mental states and act intentionally. The following clinical example illustrates how the clinician's theory organizes our thoughts and perceptions of a patient's symptoms as he/she contemplates the transformation of the patient's symptoms into symbolic, self-reflective thoughts so that the patient and therapist are no longer trapped in the fog of concrete repetitive experiences.

CLINICAL ILLUSTRATION

The following clinical illustration provides an opportunity to think about how a patient's presenting problem, typically a symptom or sign, becomes expanded through being viewed through a theoretical lens as a symbol which carries a series of meanings which unconsciously organize his/her life. A patient began therapy telling me that his wife found sexual texts on his cell phone, a series of intense sexual conversations and pictures between himself and a woman colleague. He says that he was both extremely ashamed and relieved after he and his wife talked about these texts and he confessed that this was not an isolated incident, that he had been texting (sexting) woman for over a decade, well before he had met his wife and they married. Over the years he would begin these texting (sexting) relationships with no conscious thought of actual physical contact, however, he said that occasionally a woman would pursue him and they would become engaged in what he described as uncomfortable sexual encounters. He spoke calmly, his presentation was remarkably free of anxiety or other indications of distress. He described his symptom as something that seemed to occur randomly, outside of his conscious control, something that he did not understand and would like to stop. He hoped that psychotherapy could help him understand and control this alien, self-destructive behavior. As a clinician and psychoanalyst my thoughts quickly move toward attempting to conceptualize this patient's self-destructive behavior; developing a preliminary set of hypotheses, a "treatment plan," a dynamic understanding of his symptom, a map which might provide a direction for the therapy relationship. I asked myself a series of questions; how is this symptom related to his early experience, what purpose does it serves in his current life, and what unarticulated desires and meanings does his repetitive, concrete, self-destructive, behavior express to himself and others.

These preliminary questions turn away from the patient's immediate concerns—his symptoms, focusing on different theories as potential maps, which will contextualize and locate these symptom in a wider set of meanings or symbols. Patients' symptoms and presenting problems can be thought of as signs that point to larger contexts through which patients develop more complex symbolic understandings of their symptoms and behavior. This transformation of concrete signs/symptoms to symbolic experience and language has been a central concept in all psychoanalytic and psychodynamic approaches to psychotherapy. One of the purposes of this book is to see the relationship between psychoanalytic, developmental, cognitive, and neuropsychological theories as overlapping maps which present different sets of coordinates through which we locate patients' presenting problems—their symptoms—in larger normative contexts.

As in most psychoanalytic and psychodynamically oriented psychotherapy this patient's symptom became an entry point expanding his understanding from an unconscious constricted pattern of living into a more extensive movement into his past, present and future. As our work progressed this patient's symptom became articulated and suggested a new context of meaning involving his inability to ask for attention and his experience of needing to keep his desires hidden. Our work involved both understanding the origins of his need to keep his desires for attention hidden within a passive schizoid shell, and helping him develop the capacity to reflect on, symbolize, and enjoy his needs and experiences for attention. This patient's difficulty in symbolizing his needs for and experiences of receiving attention dominated his personal relationships with his wife and his work life where he had felt stuck and unable to make progress.

OVERVIEW

This book develops themes associated with the movement from concrete symptoms, signs, to the development of the capacity to create meaning, through symbolization and self-reflective thought. The first two chapters are largely theoretical and describe the evolution of psychoanalytic theory, developmental, cognitive, and neuropsychology. I present overlapping and parallel concepts and highlight the synergistic potential of integrating similar concepts and concerns from psychoanalytic, developmental, cognitive, and neuropsychological approaches to the mind and behavior. One dimension of these multiple approaches to the mind is the recognition that the mind does not operate as a hierarchical structure but is organized as parallel systems within which sensations and perceptions about the external world are apprehended, organized, and meanings generated differently from the sensations and perceptions about the inner world of subjective relationships. There is agreement among these transformational theories that the mind as generated within social or more accurately intersubjective contexts of close relationships in families and psychotherapy.

The next three chapters focus on the development of symbolization, the creation of meaning, within the clinical realms of psychoanalysis and psychotherapy. These three chapters address the use of dreams, humor, and pleasure within clinical work in order to illustrate aspects of the development of the capacity for symbolization and mentalization. In these chapters two forms of interpretation are described: traditional discursive, asymmetrical interpretations which provide explanations for behavior and symmetrical, non-discursive, presentational interpretations which generate emotional experiences, identifications, and more metaphoric processes in generating meaning in psychoanalysis and psychotherapy.

The following two chapters present a normative understanding of the difficulty in facilitating change in psychotherapy and psychoanalysis. Psychotherapy and psychoanalysis are often presented as a relatively easy process; these two chapters present the difficulty therapists have in maintaining their ability to think and be emotionally present with patients who have dissociative experiences often reporting extremely concrete, superficial, or self-destructive behaviors. In the work with these patients there is an ongoing sequence of breakdown and repair in which the capacity for symbolization collapses and the transference countertransference relationship becomes experienced as too real. The next chapter continues the themes developed in the two previous chapters but focuses on the supervisory process. Supervision is described as having both discursive or educational and procedural aspects, as well as involving important elements of procedural learning. This chapter brings together concepts of implicit and procedural learning from cognitive and neuropsychological theories with psychoanalytic concepts in developing a constructive, trustworthy supervisory relationship. The last chapter highlights the similarities among psychoanalytic, developmental, cognitive, and neuropsychological approaches and focuses on the evolving concepts of embodied cognition, embodied metaphors, and the use of poetic-like experiences in the development of the capacity for symbolic thought and mentalization.

Chapter One

From Sign to Symbol

The Evolution of Psychoanalysis from a Search For Truth to the Creation of Meaning

Psychoanalytic theory has been continuously evolving from Freud's early collaboration with Breuer (Breuer & Freud, 1893) through the present. Discussions of the evolving nature of psychoanalysis are often presented as partisan debates (Blass, 2010a, 2010b) which attempt to define "what psychoanalysis is." Rather than entering this futile argument, I prefer to view psychoanalysis as a living system, evolving sometimes smoothly, integrating past clinical and theoretical perspectives, and sometimes disrupted by new ideas reflecting challenges presented by current scientific and cultural thought. Several authors (Hamilton, 1993; Hanly, 1990) in discussing differences and similarities among psychoanalytic theories suggest two basic dimensions: correspondence which emphasizes the theory's relationship with knowable external events, and coherence which emphasizes the theory's ability to make consistent meaning conceptually and clinically. In this book I emphasize a coherence model of psychoanalytic theory and practice. I believe that what is largely knowable and teachable in psychoanalysis are the underlying theoretical and clinical models which reflect both internal coherence and the scientific and cultural zeitgeist in which each theory developed.

Freud's simple description of psychoanalysis as the "talking cure" anchored it firmly in the world of language, signs, and symbols. His revolutionary case studies described conversations through which his patients moved beyond their experiences of distress (their symptoms) understood as signs that pointed to more complex symbolic narratives of forgotten childhood experiences and intolerable wishes. While a focus on symbolic transformation has been its core, the nature of this transformational process has evolved from Freud's positivist perspective, to the pragmatic perspective of interpersonal and relational psychoanalysis and to the postmodern, constructivist perspectives of object relations and Lacanian theory. These three perspectives represent different periods in the scientific and cultural zeitgeist of psychoanalysis, different approaches to the practice of psychotherapy and supervision, and different approaches to the transformation of concrete signs and symptoms to symbolic experience.

Classical psychoanalysis, interpersonal/relational psychoanalysis, and object relations theory represent shifting algorithms within psychoanalysis's past, present, and future; however, they also represent multiple dimensions of the complex activity of clinical psychoanalysis experienced in the moment to moment choices which occur in any treatment. Each theory describes how the mind transforms concrete symptoms, experiences, behaviors, impulses, memories, persistent problems, and relationship difficulties into symbolic thought, intentions, and experiences of identity which provide a subjective sense of being a person who can say "this is me." Each theory emphasizes different content, different views of mental health, psychopathology, and how psychoanalysis and psychotherapy transforms concrete signs into symbols.

Freud was gifted in the use of metaphors to describe the complex explicit and implicit transformational processes within psychoanalysis. In describing the complex process of psychoanalysis he first suggested the metaphor of a surgeon, then a general, and finally a detective. Each metaphor altered the algorithm of psychoanalysis, changing the rules of the game, including the concepts of cure, growth and the process of transformation. With a wink to Dickens's *A Christmas Carol*, I will describe three literary metaphors, like Scrooge's dream of Marlowe's ghost, to track the evolving process of transforming signs to symbols in the evolution of psychoanalysis. These literary metaphors embody different perspectives on psychoanalysis's past, present, and future. Sherlock Holmes, the rational, objective detective/scientist in search of hidden truths, represents the Freudian and ego psychological positivist perspective. Sir Lancelot, the flawed hero, conscious of how his/her subjectivity influences his/her perception of the patient, the transference-countertransference relationship, represents an interpersonal/relational, pragmatic perspective. The Wizard of Oz, who creates illusions and metaphoric enactments, facilitates the patient's development of the capacity to symbolize their concrete experience, represents the postmodern perspectives of object relations, phenomenological, and Lacanian theories.

FREUD: THE SEARCH FOR HIDDEN TRUTH

Freud developed psychoanalysis in the late nineteenth century as a way to treat patients' neurological-like symptoms which did not fit the then current neurological and anatomical knowledge. The inability to find physical explanations for these symptoms reaffirmed the prevailing view that neurotic patients were either morally or physically weak.[1] Freud did not accept this view; his strong positivist and humanistic values insisted that all things have knowable causes and his commitment to humanism and the romantic tradition (Szasz, 1974; Fromm, 1970) valued all people, including the marginalized neurotics and the devalued women. Through his persistent study, Freud came to understand that his patients' symptoms were unsymbolized expressions of forbidden impulses, signs that pointed to unacceptable wishes and memories of emotionally painful events. Freud (Breuer & Freud, 1893) encouraged patients to "free associate," to speak with as little restraint and concern for social conventions as possible. Through this newly designed process of verbal exchange (Khan, 1973) Freud could connect his patient's symptom with "forgotten" painful memories which had been expressed as involuntary symptoms and behaviors, as signs which pointed to some "forgotten" or repressed memories.

Freud (Breuer & Freud, 1893; Freud, 1925) generalized his treatment experiences into a model of the mind organized around the separation of words or symbols, from memories and symptoms or signs. He found that when patients were encouraged to speak in an unguarded manner they would describe the context in which their symptoms first occurred, which allowed him to interpret, describe, reconstruct, and symbolize the forgotten feelings, wishes, and events. This search for hidden truth, the recovery of memories from the past (Freud, 1920, 1937), and the development of insight into the forgotten truth has remained the core concept of therapeutic action in classical psychoanalysis and ego psychology.

Freud presented his early case of Katrina (Breuer & Freud, 1893) as an illustration of his theory of repressed sexual trauma as the origin of neurotic symptoms. This early case, which seems more like a schematic diagram, provides a simple model for Freud's concept of the relationship between signs and symbols, symptoms, and forgotten events. Freud's presentation of this material is charming and strategic, supporting Freud's developing view that sexual impulses and wishes caused the disruption in representation or symbolization, the linking of words with memories, which result in hysterical symptoms. Katrina was a young woman who worked at a mountain inn where Freud was vacationing. He noticed that she acted oddly and seemed unhappy. He reports the following conversation which can be read like a psychotherapy transcript.

"Well, what is it you suffer from?"

"I get so out of breath. Not always. But sometimes it catches me so that I think I shall suffocate."

This did not, at first sight, sound like a nervous symptom. But soon it occurred to me that probably it was only a description that stood for an anxiety attack: she was choosing shortness of breath out of the complex of sensations arising from anxiety and laying undue stress on that single factor. (pp. 125–126)

Was I to make an attempt at an analysis? I could not venture to transplant hypnosis to these altitudes, but perhaps I might succeed with a simple talk. I should have to try a lucky guess. I had found often enough that in girls, anxiety was a consequence of the horror by which a virginal mind is overcome when it is faced for the first time with the world of sexuality.

So I said: "If you don't know, I'll tell you how I think you got your attacks. At that time, two years ago, you must have seen or heard something that very much embarrassed you, and that you'd much rather not have seen."

"Heavens, yes!" she replied, "that was when I caught my uncle with the girl, with Franziska, my cousin." (p. 127)

"Then why were you so frightened when you found them together? Did you understand it? Did you know what was going on?"

"Oh no. I didn't understand anything at that time. I was only sixteen. I don't know what I was frightened about." (p. 128)

After this, however, to my astonishment she dropped these threads and began to tell me two sets of older stories, which went back two or three years earlier than the traumatic moment. The first set related to occasions on which the same uncle had made sexual advances to her herself, when she was only fourteen years old. (p. 129)

Immediately she had finished this set of memories she began to tell me a second set, which dealt with occasions on which she had noticed something between her uncle and Franziska. (p. 130)

At the end of these two sets of memories she came to a stop. She was like someone transformed. The sulky, unhappy face had grown lively, her eyes were bright, she was lightened and exalted. Meanwhile the understanding of her case had become clear to me. The later part of what she had told me, in an apparently aimless fashion, provided an admirable explanation of her behaviour at the scene of the discovery. At that time she had carried about with her two sets of experiences which she remembered but did not understand, and from which she drew no inferences. When she caught sight of the couple in intercourse, she at once established a connection between the new impression and these two sets of recollections, she began to understand them and at the same time to fend them off. There then followed a short period of working-out, of 'incubation', after which the symptoms of conversion set in, the vomiting as a substitute for moral and physical disgust. This solved the riddle. She had not been disgusted by the sight of the two people but by the memory which that sight had stirred up in her. And, taking everything into account, this could only be the memory of the attempt on her at night when she had "felt her uncle's body."

So when she had finished her confession I said to her: "I know now what it was you thought when you looked into the room. You thought: 'Now he's doing with her what he wanted to do with me that night and those other times.' That was what you were disgusted at, because you remembered the feeling when you woke up in the night and felt his body."

"It may well be," she replied, "that that was what I was disgusted at and that that was what I thought." (p. 131)

Thus the case was cleared up. But stop a moment! What about the recurrent hallucination of the head, which appeared during her attacks and struck terror into her? Where did it come from? I proceeded to ask her about it, and, as though her knowledge, too, had been extended by our conversation, she promptly replied: "Yes, I know now. The head is my uncle's head I recognize it now but not from that time. Later, when all the disputes had broken out, my uncle gave way to a senseless rage against me. He kept saying that it was all my fault: if I hadn't chattered, it would never have come to a divorce. He kept threatening he would do something to me; and if he caught sight of me at a distance his face would get distorted with rage and he would make for me with his hand raised. I always ran away from him, and always felt terrified that he would catch me some time unawares. The face I always see now is his face when he was in a rage." (p. 132)

Freud (Breuer & Freud, 1893, p. 132) concludes his discussion of this case by presenting a dynamic theory of the relationship between experience and memory; "(I)n every analysis of a case of hysteria based on sexual traumas we find that impressions from the pre-sexual period, which produced no effect on the child, attain traumatic power at a later date as memories, when the girl or married woman has acquired an understanding of sexual life."

As Freud's clinical work evolved he came to see that patients often did not want to give up their symptoms and resisted his wish to be the helpful doctor. These clinical observations led to the development of the structural model of the mind in which resistance, repression, and defense were active elements defining the dynamic unconscious (Freud, 1923) now suggested that the analyst should be like a general, alert in the battle with the patient's resistance, changing the metaphor for psychoanalysis from a simple medical procedure to a prolonged struggle with a fierce enemy. Freud's (1909) third metaphor, Sherlock Holmes, suggested that like the great nineteenth century detective, analysts' persistent, deductive, rational inquiry brings to light the patient's hidden truths and forgotten crimes. This shift moved the analytic relationship from one of a battle to that of a collaboration in which the discovery of the unconscious meanings would allow the patient to become free from their repetitive symptoms and behaviors.

This third position is illustrated in a letter to Jung. Freud (1909) discusses an interaction with M. Spielrein, in which his use of the metaphor of Sherlock Holmes illustrates his (Freud, 1920) growing emphasis on the transformation of passively experienced repetitive trauma through simple interpretations, into an active collaborative relationship in which the patient comes to recognize him/herself as a responsible agent through bringing hidden truths into the light of day.

> Fräulein Spielrein has admitted in her second letter that her business has to do with you; apart from that, she has not disclosed her intentions. My reply was ever so wise and penetrating; I made it appear as though the most tenuous of clues had enabled me Sherlock Holmes-like to guess the situation (which of course was none too difficult after your communications) and suggested a more appropriate procedure, something endopsychic, as it were. Whether it will be effective, I don't know. But now I must entreat you, don't go too far in the direction of contrition and reaction. (pp. 234–235)

In this brief communication, which refers to Jung's affair with Spielrein, Freud metaphorizes the analyst's position in the implicit structure of the analytic relationship, reframing the psychoanalytic method, emphasizing the process of inquiry over battle. The psychoanalyst's role evolved from a surgeon, to that of a general, to a clever detective who uncovers forgotten crimes and hidden truths, helping the patient take responsibility for his/her disowned actions. Freud's reconceptualization of psychoanalytic action emphasizes the patient's movement from unconscious or disowned experiences (Schafer, 1976), passively experienced as events in the external world, to the recognition of unconscious wishes and truths, which are at the root of the patient's unhappiness and self-destructive choices. Freud's idea of making the unconscious conscious, of the ego and secondary process rational thought dominating the id and primary process thought, are embodied in the metaphor of the analyst as detective. This metaphor also reflected the zeitgeist of positivism which put a premium on defeating the irrational impulses of man, the importance of making rational choices, and the translation of symptoms and signs into narrative, historical explanations in which the present was always a reflection of the past.

THE EXPANSION OF EXPERIENCE: INTERPERSONAL AND RELATIONAL PSYCHOANALYSIS

In the middle of the twentieth century psychoanalysis's emphasis on positivism expanded into a pragmatic perspective, which shifted the model of the mind from a hierarchical system analogized as an archeological site, to one governed by purpose, a functional system. The pragmatic approach developed in interpersonal psychoanalysis, influenced by Peirce, Dewey, and William James, reconceptualized the mind as a purposeful system in which signs and symbols have differential abilities to communicate and organize information. The pragmatic perspective shifted our understanding of the transformation of signs to symbols from questions of origins, what past experience particular signs stood for, to questions of purpose, how does a particular sign organize experience and what is the purpose of repetitive symptomatic behaviors. Interpersonal and relational psychoanalysis developed within this pragmatic perspective emphasizing the demystification of seemingly purposeless, painful experience and expanding the individual's psychological world through new experiences within the therapeutic relationship.

Interpersonal and relational psychoanalysis redefined concepts of structure, psychological development, psychopathology, and the nature of therapeutic action. These theories rejected Freud's one person intrapsychic focus, developing a two person interpersonal perspective. Psychopathology was thought of as an individual's desperate attempts to maintain attachment and security, clinging to childhood patterns, traumas, and beliefs in the analytic as well as in other relationships. Interpersonal psychoanalysis developed a more active approach of inquiry, viewing the analyst as a participant observer always bringing his/her personal perspectives into the transference countertransference experiences. Levenson (1972) described the inevitability of becoming trapped within these transference countertransference structures and the importance of the analyst's first person experience as a participant which provided a critical opportunity to work out these complex transference countertransference enactments between patient and therapist in the here and now. From a somewhat different perspective Gabbard and Westen (2003) drew attention to three main themes concerning the therapeutic action of psychoanalysis: a) the reduced importance of interpretation compared to the relationship as such and the acknowledgment of a multiplicity of modes for a therapeutic action of psychoanalysis; b) a shift of the emphasis from reconstruction to construction in the here and now of the session; and c) the importance of negotiation of the therapeutic atmosphere created between analyst and patient. For these authors, the insight reached through interpretation and the transformations which can be obtained through the relational experience work in synergy. In fact, the emphasis on reconstruction has in recent years considerably decreased, in favor of the interaction in the here and now of the session, allowing the patient to gain an insight into the influences of the past on his present conflicts and object relations (Arlow, 1987; Gabbard, 1997).

Relational analysts (Mitchell, 1991; Aron, 1992a, 1992b; Renik, 1995) expanded this emphasis on the interpersonal interaction, emphasizing the analyst's subjectivity, personal history, the importance of self-disclosure, and the therapeutic benefits of new relational experiences in the analytic dyad where the analyst functions (Burke, 1992) as both a new object and a traditional transference object. As a new object the analyst provides novel positive experiences which contrasts with the patient's earlier experiences with their historical objects. These new implicit and explicit experiences facilitate the development of new relational schemas, freeing the patient from the repetitions of past symptomatic behaviors. Often the analyst becomes entangled in an enactment, unwittingly acting out aspects of the transference countertransference relationship and rupturing the therapeutic harmony. These inevitable ruptures typically become repaired as the analyst recognizes his/her subjective and personal contribution to the transference countertransference difficulties. These repeating experiences of rupture and repair often involve the analyst's self-disclosure, deepening the sense of mutual knowing, fostering greater freedom and intimacy in the analytic relationship.

The narrative of many cases presented by interpersonal and relational analysts (Mitchell, 1991; Gerson, 1996; Summers, 2013) present a romantic perspective (Newirth, 2014), describing patients as victims of abusive or negligent parents, having suffered childhood trauma, including sexual or physical abuse. If the literary genre of classical psychoanalysis was the detective novel, the literary genre of interpersonal and relational psychoanalysis is the romantic, adventure novel, in which a flawed hero, the analyst, rescues the trapped, damaged, and emotionally stunted victim, the patient. Clinical illustrations often emphasize patients' and analysts' struggles with their inner demons, the powerful hold of the traumatic events of the past, and the fear that accompanies this mutual journey into new uncharted experiences. I think of Sir Lancelot, the imperfect knight of King Arthur's Round Table, as a metaphor that represents the romantic and heroic struggles described in these case histories, where the analyst, after confronting his/her own demons and personal failures, slays the dragon, freeing the patient from the prisons of the past. Like the Sir Lancelot legend, analysis becomes a trial for both analyst and patient (Davies, 1998), as each struggles with the multiple self-states that both analyst and patient bring into the transference countertransference relationship.

SIR LANCELOT: THE ANALYST AS FLAWED HERO

Jessica Benjamin's (2009) paper on the necessity of acknowledging failure illustrates the implicit and explicit struggles of the analyst, a flawed hero like Sir Lancelot, who frees the patient from the repetitions of the past through a series of personal encounters. Benjamin (2009) describes her work with Hannah, emphasizing her patient's childhood experiences of maternal failure and her own struggle to not to enter into the more traditional role of the interpreting analyst, Sherlock Holmes, emphasizing truth over experience. Benjamin's paper allows us to understand the analyst's experience of choosing between being a new object in contrast to a traditional transference object, and the difficult task of maintaining her position as a new object, providing new relational experience within the transference countertransference relationship. I think of this approach as a romantic, heroic relationship, in which the analyst rescues the patient from a traumatic and dangerous past through her presence as a different person, providing reparative experiences, encouraging the patient to accept being a more authentic, albeit flawed self, much like the analyst.

Benjamin (2009, p. 446) illustrates her struggle to be a soothing maternal presence and neither interpret the transference, or become emotionally disregulated as did the patient's mother, who failed to survive Hannah's affective storms. Being a new object disconfirmed Hannah's certainty that the other "would be crushed by her destructive disappointment; and that she must protect that other/mother by showing herself to be unworthy. Thus she experienced herself as the destructive one who kept ruining a potential viable third." Benjamin describes a particular moment as a personal failure, losing her place as a thoughtful relational analyst providing new soothing experiences. Responding out of frustration and anger, she describes a moment as becoming an "authentic" self. I put "authentic" in quotation marks because it represents a shift in the analyst's position from being a new analytic object into being a person (Benjamin, 2000), a flawed hero, unadorned by theory. Benjamin (2009, p. 447) comments that she speaks as if Hannah were her own daughter and questioned why "she thought her anxiety and vulnerability were so unacceptable, why weren't they a part of imperfect but acceptable humanness?" Although Benjamin describes this as an analytic failure, the patient experiences Benjamin heroically, as her "staunch defender," rescuing her from being trapped in her repetitive self-disparaging behaviors. From a more traditional perspective, the patient's approving response may be thought of as repeating an old transference pattern in which she protects the analyst as she did her mother; however, this possibility was not explored, perhaps because of Benjamin's emphasis on the experiential dimension of the relationship rather than on discovering hidden meaning in repetitive transference experiences.

Benjamin describes a second moment of failure, becoming trapped in an enactment in which she becomes angry with Hannah who describes herself as an incompetent mother. Benjamin describes the value of this enactment as she and the patient work out their multiple self experiences, showing how the inevitable processes of rupture and repair are critical aspects in the development of new analytic experiences and growth. Throughout this enactment, Benjamin remains a person, eschewing efforts at interpretation and simply being a flawed hero, Sir Lancelot. Benjamin consistently emphasizes her role as a new object, often experiencing herself as an authentic person, sometimes flawed and sometimes heroic, but always in an experience near encounter with the patient. If the classical position emphasized the discovery of hidden truths and forgotten crimes, the relational position redefines therapeutic action as repeating experiences of rescue, rupture, and repair, of the encounter between the flawed patient and the flawed analyst; the meeting between Guinevere and Sir Lancelot.

TRANSFORMATIONAL PERSPECTIVES: CREATING MEANING

Toward the end of the twentieth century transformational models emerged in psychoanalysis (Bion, 1965), developmental psychology (Piaget, 1973), and neuropsychology (Schore, 2003a, 2003b; Solms, 2003) which focused on the individual's ability to represent and symbolize experience, to make meaning, rather than on the discovery of disowned and repressed wishes, unacknowledged actions, or attempts to repair repetitive, self-destructive relationship patterns. These theories present similar models of the mind describing the development of structures that allow the individual to transform concrete, action oriented experiences into complex symbols and narratives. These transformational models suggest that meaning is created differently in two experiential realms, the external world of things and objects and the internal affective world of personal relationships. Psychoanalytic theorists (Ferro, 2006; Grotstein, 2007; Newirth, 2003; Ogden, 2010; Riolo, 2007; Symington, 2007) associated with transformational models have extended Bion's and Winnicott's theories of symbolization, reverie, and transitional experience, focusing on facilitating the development of the patient's capacity to make meaning and develop the capacity for symbolic thought. This model contrasts with traditional hierarchical models in which meaning and memories are lost through repression and recovered through an interpretive process, or the interpersonal-relational model in which meanings are developed through expanding experience and encounters which disconfirm older scripts and introduce new relational experiences.

Patients who are unable to function in the intersubjective world of relationships and generate symbolic, subjective meaning organize experience concretely, typically locating thoughts and experience in the external world of facts and authority, rather than as products of their own or another's mind. Unable to create intersubjective meaning, they organize experience concretely through action, are flooded by affect, and represent experience in modes of psychic (Fonagy et al., 2003) or symbolic (Segal, 1978) equivalence as absolutely real. Grotstein (1995) refers to patients who are unable to symbolize personal experience and are trapped in an external world of impersonal meaning as "Orphans of the Real." In this concrete mode: I am what I am, you are what you are, and everything will always be the same.

THE WIZARD OF OZ: THE DEVELOPMENT OF SYMBOLIZATION

The Wizard of Oz is a literary metaphor for the psychoanalytic experience in the transformational model. The Wizard of Oz is a representation of the literary genre of magical realism found in both adult's and children's literature which present the fears and struggles which inhabit our lives and the unconscious in dream-like narratives of transformation. In the Wizard of Oz, Dorothy, in a dream-like state, is transported by a tornado to the Land of Oz where we follow her desperate attempts to return home. This symptom, her persistent attempts to return home, is a sign that points to her confusion, lack of direction, adolescent anxiety, being orphaned, and her struggles with loved and hated maternal objects; the bad witch who she destroys and the good witch who helps her on her way. In order to return home,[2] she is told to get help from the Wizard of Oz, the one who is supposed to know, and who she believes will help her find her way home. On the way to Oz she meets three fellow travelers, the Scarecrow, the Tin Man, and the Cowardly Lion, and invites them to join her on her journey with the promise that the Wizard will help each of them become the person he/she dreams of becoming.

The Wizard of Oz[3] does not function as a detective finding hidden truths and forgotten crimes, or as a flawed hero rescuing or repairing an injured patient through new emotional, affirmative experiences; rather he is a kind of actor, creating illusions (Winnicott, 1971a; Symington, 2007) which transform patients' concrete paranoid experiences into symbolic subjective experiences. Like Dorothy, we become angry with the Wizard when the screen is pulled away and we see that he is simply a man who creates illusions and does not have special abilities and knowledge. Our anger reflects our disappointment that the analyst does not know what we wish he knew, and cannot act in the way we hoped he could.

Lacan (2007) similarly describes the analyst as being "the one who is supposed to know." This view of the analyst, that he/she is the one who is supposed to know, highlights the question of who knows and who pretends to know, or who doesn't know and who pretends to not know. For Lacan, the patient believes that the analyst knows the way the patient can resolve his/her problems in living, or that he/she knows the truth that the patient fears knowing. The analyst knows that he/she does not know how the patient should live, while also knowing that within the evolving transference countertransference relationship, the possibility will present itself for the patient to become more fully himself and metaphorize his experience so that he may live more fully in the intersubjective symbolic world. From the transformational perspective, the therapist/analyst is only able to help the patient generate symbolic, transitional experiences, develop metaphors that integrate and symbolize fearful disowned and desired experiences: a diploma for the Scarecrow so that he can know his intelligence, a Valentine heart for the Tin

Man, so that he can know his capacity to feel and love, a medal for the lion so that he can puff out his chest, roaring his presence and know his courage, and ruby slippers, so that Dorothy can experience her power to return home. These symbolic or metaphoric enactments are not superficial carnival tricks; they are deeply saturated, presentational symbols (Langer, 1942) that involve complex developmental, self-reflective experiences, increased capacity for symbolization, mentalization, and the continuous creative internal conversations involved in reverie and dreaming.

CLINICAL ILLUSTRATION: I WANT A PENIS

The following case illustrates the transformational model of psychoanalysis. I will present four moments[4] in my work with a long term analytic patient which illustrate the metaphorization and transformation of a significant disowned aspect of the patient's experience which had been expressed concretely in frequent painful, repetitive experiences in her life. I had been working with Holly for many years during which time she resolved much of her early depression, substantially improved her relationship with her husband, helped launch her children into self-directed and successful careers, expanded her sense of herself from that of a depressed maternal caretaker developing a more complex life as a woman, an academic, and a person able to stand up for herself. Early in our work we focused on her fearfulness of entering or engaging the world; this anxiety had a generalized phobic quality, and was concretely expressed as a "fear of flying." This phobic attitude toward the world had been significantly resolved and resulted in Holly's being able, among other things, to enter into a graduate program in which she succeeded and received the recognition that had been missing earlier in her life. However, like many people, the necessity to complete her thesis resulted in a return of her phobic orientation and an inability to complete this final step.

Holly had a long standing fantasy of having either a radio or television show where she would facilitate discussions between children and adults. However, she has been afraid to pursue or create the opportunities to make her fantasy into a reality. In our work we identified her fear of being seen, her anxiety about her exhibitionistic wishes, and her difficulty separating from and competing with her sisters. It is not clear whether her fearful experience of having a radio or television show is only a concrete expression of her desire to be seen, to have a voice, to stand out, to differentiate herself from her mother and her three older sisters, or an unconscious exhibitionistic wish that stands behind her phobic attitude toward the world, inhibiting her forward progress. The following four moments illustrate the progressive symbolization of an important and disowned aspect of Holly's unconscious organization of her experience of herself in the world.

Several years ago, Holly was awakened by an anxiety filled dream in which she was a lawyer, dressed in a sophisticated Armani suit, and as she began to present the closing arguments of her case, she became paralyzed and could not speak. In talking about the dream, we focused on the suit, which she recalled as navy blue, fitted and very elegant—something that she would never own. It became clear that being seen in this very grown up way was extremely frightening, bringing up memories of her childhood and a sense that she should always be the little sister "sitting in the back seat of the car" on family trips. In working with this dream we developed an evocative metaphor for her conflicted feelings about being seen; a red Armani suit, which expressed both her fear of being seen and her desire to stand out.

At another point in the analysis, Holly had a dream, which she initially felt too embarrassed to talk about. In this dream she was about to perform, to sing in public; the setting was unclear but the excitement was palpable. As she held the microphone up to sing it became a penis. She froze in the dream and felt embarrassed thinking about the multiple sexual meanings of the dream. We spoke about many possible interpretations of this dream. One obvious classical interpretation was about penis envy, her inability to accept herself as a woman and her denied castration anxiety. A more contemporary interpretation was that the dream reflected unspoken aspects of the transference countertransference relationship which involved her and/or my unspoken sexual desires. An alternative interpersonal interpretation was that like other men, I could not tolerate her having her own, independent voice and would overwhelm her sexually, putting her in her place. Another interpretation which seemed more relational was that in becoming a woman she had to give up her own voice, to castrate herself, become a female eunuch (Greer, 1970). All of these interpretations were plausible and reflected different psychoanalytic perspectives. However, what seemed new in this dream, and in our work on it, was not the sexual tension and reverie that was present and had frequently come into the foreground in our transference countertransference relationship, but rather her equating her voice, her ability to speak with a penis, or perhaps more exactly with the absence of a penis. It was as if Holly, like the Scarecrow in the Wizard of Oz who sang the song if I only had a brain, dreamt that she was singing her own song, if I only had a penis, in order to articulate her lack of a capacity to have a voice of her own, to be fully alive.

Holly's dream suggests interesting questions about how we think of sexual dreams, such as Holly's dream of the microphone becoming a penis. It seems to me that contemporary American psychoanalysis has interpreted sexual content, like the penis in Holly's dream, in two ways, as a literal sexual object representing a repressed wish/experience or as an abstract cultural experience; as either an erotic desire/fear or as an experience of gender, power, domination and submission. Lacan adds another perspective to the discussion of sexual symbols. Lacan (2007) differentiates the concept of the penis from that of the phallic object. The penis is a reference to an actual body part, and the phallus or phallic object reflects the movement from concrete, immature forms of thinking focused on images (the mirror stage), to the capacity to use language, to be part of the symbolic order, including experiences of subjective desire, and the recognition of loss and absence. Lacan's differentiation of the penis from the phallus describes the difference between concrete experience of actual body parts and the symbolic meaning of metaphorical objects. For Lacan the phallus, or phallic object, is a metaphor representing a movement from the mirror stage in which the individual concretely wants to see him/herself puffed up, larger than life, dependent on others' affirmation, to the symbolic mode where the person struggles to use words and metaphors to express his/her desire while recognizing that words always fall short. Lacan (2007) describes this process of transformation from signs to symbols as "traversing the fantasy," which involves the symbolic recognition that we are the authors of our own lives. From a Lacanian perspective, my patient's dream may not simply be a dream about erotic desire in the transference countertransference relationship or our gendered power dynamics, but her wish to have her own phallus, a wish to enter into the symbolic order where she can speak, articulate her desire, have her own voice, and be able to metaphorize her anxiety about being seen and heard, to go beyond the limits imposed by her concrete experience of family and culture.

Holly's mother died about a year ago, at an advanced age, having survived several major illnesses and two husbands. Her father died many years before when she was a late adolescent. Holly had surprised herself, taking the lead in arranging care for her mother during this illness which lasted several months. Holly spent a lot of time with her mother, recognizing that her mother's inability to know, or want to know, about her illness, recapitulated her difficulty knowing her own and her children's feelings, her inability to express emotions, particularly sad, depressed feelings of loss. Holly felt particularly good about her ability to know her own feelings and deal with the sadness and loss of her mother.

About four months after Holly's mother's death the following event occurred. She arrived for a session and with a combination of excitement and vigilance said: "I want a penis." She described how she had been thinking about getting a "penis" and that she really wanted to do it. Her affect felt as if she was about to embark on an adventure. When I asked about this she elaborated her thoughts, her fantasy, in an unusually unembarrassed way. She wanted to get a strap on penis, she wanted to know what it felt like to have this appendage, she wanted to look at herself in the mirror, she wanted to wear it under her clothes in public so that only she knew about it, she discussed it with her husband and suggested that she might like to use it in their sexual relationship. She wondered if this meant that she wanted to be a lesbian, and felt that was not where she was at. She wanted to have a penis that she could play with in all possible ways, and to know what it feels like to have a penis.

I found myself propelled simultaneously into many thoughts and reveries by Holly's straightforward statement of her desire for a penis. First, my old psychoanalytic superego came to the fore; it felt threatened, demanded an interpretation, stating that we had come to the ultimate truth, penis envy and castration anxiety. Second, my relational self came to the fore, believing that this must reflect some unknown part of myself, a personal failure which I needed to identify, talk about repair, and then rescue Holly from her wish to act out. Lastly, I felt inquisitive and wanted to join Holly in this new playful experience, imagining what it would be like for her and imagining her being in various places wearing and being aware of her penis, including in sessions with me. My response, which somewhat surprised me, was to ask Holly if she knew where to get a penis and then telling her about a store that I had often passed which specialized in erotic toys for women. Rather than interpreting and searching for some repressed oedipal wish or focusing on our immediate encounter, I seemed to be reacting in a playful way, seeing and experiencing her desire for a penis as a transitional object. The session continued in a playful way, it felt warm, and like with other transitional experiences, it was not possible to say whether we were talking about reality or creating a dreamlike space that Holly and I could inhabit together.

I believe that the patient playfully introducing her wish to have a penis was an invitation to develop a transitional experience around the central themes of her phobic anxiety, of being seen and heard and of power which was encoded in her familial and cultural experiences of gender. Throughout Holly's treatment, fears of separation, of standing apart from her sisters and mother, of being seen, of being heard and of being free, have been experienced as concrete realities, in modes of psychic equivalents as absolute truth, as facts, rather than symbolically as thoughts, scripts, symbols, or laws that must be followed or could be transgressed. Although we may think that Holly's penis represented a concrete experience of gender and power, I see it as a movement into a metaphorical experience, using a strap on penis as a presentational symbol, a metaphor, like a performance artist uses objects to express deep affective, symbolic meanings in shocking and humorous ways. I think of this metaphoric enactment as illustrating the difference between the functional and symbolic use of objects, as the difference between tools and toys, as the difference between work and play.

Discussions of the development of the capacity for symbolic experience are often difficult and confusing because we are not used to thinking about representational activity as having different psychological qualities and as occurring in parallel universes of external and internal space. In most parts of her life Holly is very capable of symbolic and abstract thought; she speaks and conducts herself as a sophisticated, competent professional. However, her persistent anxiety and her phobic attitude toward speaking, being seen, and following her desires suggest that there are unconscious limits in her ability to be the author of her own life. Although our work included interpretation, articulating memories and forgotten truths, and many of the interpersonal and relational processes described above, I believe this process of progressive symbolization was a critical feature of our work. I would like to use the four moments from my work with Holly to illustrate the process of progressive symbolization and metaphorization which are central to the transformational model of therapeutic action.

Each of the analytic moments can be thought of as part of a progressive movement from an externalized, concrete, and phobic experience of herself as a passive actor toward an internal, metaphoric, and symbolic experience of herself as an empowered subject. Her fear of flying may be understood as a concrete and externalized phobic experience of personal excitement, pleasure, and power in the exploration of herself and the world. Her dream of being a well-dressed attorney paralyzed when she was about to speak and be seen suggests an internalization of her experience of personal excitement, pleasure, and power as she moves from an externalized phobic orientation to a fear of her own capacities which she can begin to challenge herself through metaphorizing this fantasy and seeing herself dressed in a red Armani suit. Her dream of a microphone turning into a penis as she is about to sing represents another movement from the more concrete internalized action which was involved in the dream of being a lawyer, to a symbolic experience of the microphone as a phallic object, something which she could potentially have and use. These shifts from concrete to symbolic representation are described by Hana Segal (1994) as a shift in attitude from treating a thought "as if" it is real to an attitude of treating a thought from the perspective of "what if" it is real. Finally Holly's wish to have a penis and my participation in this transitional experience reflected her ability to experience her penis, her phallus, more fully as a symbol and metaphor, as a toy that she could play with, a transitional experience that she can own. This transitional experience represents her increasing capacity for symbolization and the development of a set of personal metaphors which allowed her to move from a phobic and powerless state to one in which she could experience herself as a powerful, playful, person, having her own mind separate from the roles given to her by her family, her culture, and her analyst.

I believe that Holly's wish to have a penis and my ability to validate her desire for a penis was a transformational moment, a metaphoric enactment of her long disowned desire to be seen, heard as a powerful and competent person. This metaphoric enactment or transitional experience developed through my joining her and telling her where she might safely go to purchase a penis, rather than interpreting her desire from either a Freudian or a relational/cultural perspective, helped her create a new symbolic experience in the dream-like world of the analytic relationship. Holly and I continued talking about her "fantasies" about her penis, and as this evolved she seemed able to become more engaged in other experiences involving potency and pleasure, such as resuming work on her thesis. I am conflicted about whether to write about whether Holly purchased her penis, or not. This conflict reflects my sense of not fulfilling aspects of my role as a psychoanalyst, defining the reality of sexual identity and discouraging acting out. However, I feel that it would be in bad faith both to Holly and to my view of psychoanalysis as a transformational process, to the Wizard of Oz, to move this subjective dream-like experience into objective reality. I believe that Holly's penis became our metaphor, a transitional experience in which we, in the safety of the illusory world of therapy, could play with her penis, now a phallic object, which allowed her to become a more complete person and to enter more fully into the symbolic world.

However, in the transitional experiences that are generated in psychoanalysis it is hard to know what is real and what is illusory; was I encouraging her acting out, supporting a denial of the painful truth of penis envy, of limitations, or denying the seriousness of her experience of being powerless and subordinated to a patriarchal order? Am I like the Wizard of Oz simply hiding behind a screen and using theatrical tricks and props, am I the one who is supposed to know and does not know, or have I/we facilitated an important transformation through developing the metaphor of Holly's penis?

In viewing psychoanalysis as an evolving theory, I have suggested three literary metaphors to highlight the evolution of different aspects of the therapeutic action of psychoanalysis: the search for hidden truth, the importance of transference countertransference experience in creating new modes of relatedness, and the development of the capacity for symbolic thought and metaphors in creating subjective meaning. Although these perspectives evolved during different historical periods and are linked with different psychoanalytic, philosophical, cultural, and scientific systems of thought, they are all elements in contemporary psychoanalytic practice. The developing transformational models in psychoanalysis, developmental psychology, and neuropsychology focus our attention on the importance of the patient's capacity to represent experience, make meaning in a symbolic, generative mode. In this clinical model enactments are not simply useful as a source of information, or as new experience, but are useful in increasing the patient's capacity for the development of metaphors which allow the patient to organize his/her life in a generative, intentional, and active way.

NOTES

1. Ibsen's plays dramatically present the various fears and prejudices of Freud's time period, the threshold of modernism.

2. Like many patients she is interested in an answer which will allow her to act, move ahead with her life.

3. Jung (1981) presented a similar view of the analyst, suggesting that the archetype for the therapist is the Trickster, the court jester, the magician, the comic, who helps the king pierce the veil of certainty, of external reality, and enter into deeper experiences of knowledge and wisdom.

4. Stern et al. (1998) describe the analytic process as made up of moments of meeting in which a critical event may happen if both analyst and patient are able to risk something new and not follow the usual patterns of relatedness.

Chapter Two

Transformational Models in Psychoanalysis: Developmental, Cognitive, and Neuropsychology

The previous chapter described the evolution and expansion of the psychoanalytic understanding of therapeutic action through three literary metaphors: Sherlock Holmes, Sir Lancelot, and the Wizard of Oz. These metaphors described the evolution of psychoanalytic theory from a narrow search for truth, to the expansion of relationship schemas through the potential of new experiences in the here and now (Blatt, 2013), and then to the creation of meaning through symbolic enactments and the development of verbal metaphors which transform concrete, action oriented unconscious organizations into vibrant, symbolic representations of self and other. In this chapter I temporarily move away from the clinical perspective of the previous chapter to an academic focus where I will describe converging conceptualizations of the mind within divergent fields of study: psychoanalysis, linguistics, cognitive, developmental, and neuropsychological science. Traditionally the development of mind, the capacity to represent experience, reflect upon and understand the self and the world, act on desires and intentions, and navigate the complex objective and subjective worlds have been treated separately by different academic disciplines. Like the proverbial six blind men attempting to describe an elephant, each academic discipline has had its own perspective, language, and systems of explanation for the relationship between brain, mind, experience, and action. There have been few attempts to integrate these multiple academic perspectives, or engage the synergistic potential of integrating multiple perspectives into a unified concept of the mind.

In this chapter I present converging and overlapping views of the mind which have emerged in different academic disciplines, each of which has reconceptualized the mind as parallel rather than hierarchical organizations, which have different rules for processing information from the inner world of sensation and emotion and the outer world of perception and experience. This view of the mind sharply contrasts with previous views of the mind as a hierarchical organization in which the higher order centers, the cerebrum or the superego, control and limit the lower levels of the brain or mind. In this emergent transformational model the parallel mental systems transform experience into representations, memory, and symbolic experience. Although each academic discipline utilizes different concepts and language, they all delineate five dimensions:

- the mind is conceptualized as nonhierarchical, multidimensional, and interactive
- multiple systems encode information and organize knowledge and experience separately for the external world of things and the internal world of emotional experience
- a social view of the mind which is dependent on intersubjective[1] experience for its development
- a developmental view of the mind as continuing to change (grow) in its capacity to represent experience, be reflective and self-reflective
- the idea that mental representations precede and are independent from the development of verbal representations and language
- the majority of experience occurs outside of awareness, is experientially unconscious, consciousness is not privileged as the essential quality of mind or maturity

CONTEMPORARY PSYCHOANALYTIC PERSPECTIVES

The traditional psychoanalytic theory of mind, of psychic structure, viewed the mind as a tripartite hierarchical structure in which the ego acted like an executive decision maker being influenced by both the id and superego. Freud (1937) emphasized this model of surface to depth describing the mind like an archeological dig in which artifacts found at different levels were organized around the core dynamic of repression. For Freud (1937), the analyst's job was to facilitate remembering past events and failing this to construct a reasonable narrative explanation of the past. Melanie Klein profoundly shifted the psychoanalytic view of mind, developing the concept of projective identification as the central dynamic process which moved the locus of emotional experience from the hierarchical view of the mind as layers of repressed memories, often presented as a dungeon-like experience of the id, to social experiences as we interact with others.[2] Klein's (Ogden, 1979) concept of projective identification implicitly suggested that the mind functions as a two person social or intersubjective structure and not simply a one person biological structure analogous to the brain.[3] She believed the infant's early experience of affect, particularly painful affects (i.e., hunger, needing to be held, feeling dirty, frustration, anger, etc.) dominate the infant's rudimentary, moment to moment sense of awareness and required that the infant find a way to get rid of painful experiences through both demanding attention from a caregiver and developing the first cognitive operations of splitting experience into good and bad, and then through projective identification, relocating it from inside me to outside me. This dual emotional and cognitive process of splitting affect and relocating experience from inside to outside (not me) allowed the infant to experience good affective states inside of the self, feeling comfort and safety, and the bad affective states as located outside, in the parent. This early experience allowed the infant to believe that it was the other who was causing the painful experience. A simple experience of projective identification is when we blame others for causing our feelings of pain, failure, and distress, and through a process like empathy, the other unconsciously or consciously feels guilty or reacts defensively with the interaction becoming a game of hot potato in which the unwanted bad or angry experience is passed back and forth. This type of experience often happens at a moment when we get a dirty look from our spouse or lover when we return home and suddenly feel guilty and defensive.

The concept of projective identification also reflects cultural and philosophical shifts in twentieth century epistemology (our mode of knowing the world), from an objective positivist approach to knowledge, to a phenomenological and subjective approach. This epistemological change happened in many cultural and academic areas in which a subjective, experiential perspective became substituted for the earlier objective, positivist perspective.[4] Projective identification is one of the central structural concepts in the evolution of Kleinian theory which has been developed by other theorists into a sophisticated intersubjective view of human relatedness. Unlike Freud's hierarchical model of the mind, the Kleinian model views the mind as a dialectical structure of two parallel and mutually interacting organizations: the paranoid schizoid and the depressive positions, which each have specific ways of processing experience, creating meaning, and organizing relationships. The paranoid position (Newirth, 2003) is organized around the social dimension of power and control, organizing experience cognitively as absolute facts (Segal, 1978) described as symbolic equivalents where the word and what it represents are experienced as the same thing. The central question from the perspective of the paranoid schizoid position is: "do I control you (it) or do you control me (it)." The depressive position involves the integration of the emotional splits which underlie the process of projective identification allowing the representations of self and other to be experienced symbolically, becoming aware of multiple possibilities, as three dimensional complex thoughts, feelings, histories, and intentions. In the depressive state the person is able to recognize himself/herself as neither all good or all bad and is able to acknowledge and take responsibility for having hurt the other which initiates processes of repair and growth.

Winnicott was strongly influenced by Klein (Grosskyrth, 1986), and believed that her theoretical language, which reflected her personal and cultural experience, limited others' ability to use her theory. He argued for analysts to find their own language to describe and use the evolving Kleinian view of the mind. Winnicott (Grosskyrth, 1986) developed in a different cultural and familial environment than did Klein, which is reflected in his descriptions of the paranoid schizoid and depressive positions. He describes the paranoid position as a position of ruthlessness, in which the individual is self-centered, demanding, and unwilling to accept the other as having a purpose other than serving his/her needs. He described the depressive position as the position of concern highlighting the development of the capacity for both knowing the other as a separate person and recognizing how we may have let the other down. In one of his last papers, Winnicott (1969) describes the individual's achievement of the position of concern through experiences of gratitude and the recognition of how a parent or therapist has sacrificed for the child or patient.

Bion, like Winnicott, extended Klein's concept of the development of mind from the concrete thought of the paranoid schizoid position to the symbolic thought of the depressive position. He also emphasized the intersubjective (social) experiential context. While Winnicott presented his ideas from experience near, developmental perspectives, describing the importance of transitional experience, Bion wrote from an abstract, theoretical perspective, describing the transformation of raw experience, beta elements, into symbolic thought, alpha process, through the intersubjective experiences of containment. Bion (1970) developed the concept of the container contained as a metaphor to describe the intersubjective process of the developing capacity to transform the painful experiences of the paranoid schizoid position to the symbolic experiences of the depressive position. In Bion's model the child or patient evacuates or projects the concrete, painful experiences from the self, experienced as absolutely real, into the mother[5] or therapist, unconsciously stating: "I am not bad, you are bad." The mother or therapist needs to be able to contain these painful, accusatory projections (feelings) and affectively elaborate and amplify these concrete experiences, moving from a state of absolute belief to a state of possibility. Segal highlights an aspect of this transformational process noting that thinking in the paranoid schizoid position involves experiencing something "as if" it is absolutely real, while in the depressive position it is experienced as "what if" this is real, emphasizing the importance of the ability to accept the possibility that a projection may be real; that is, "what if I am a bad parent, a bad therapist." From the intersubjective perspective of the container—contained model, the critical factor is the mother's or therapist's ability to accept, tolerate, and affectively elaborate the child's or patient's conscious and unconscious projections. The parent or therapist who is not able to function as a secure container, which I describe in a later chapter as the broken container, experiences a great deal of persecutory anxiety, feeling that a present moment represents a dangerous crisis and blames the child or patient in a secondary act of projective identification, accusing the other of being bad, thoughtless, mean, which often devolves into an oscillating paranoid series of mutual blame.

Winnicott (1971a) also presented a radical two person approach to the mind, emphasizing the importance of the paradox inherent in intersubjective experiences of not being able to be certain who, where, and when a particular symbolic experience was engendered. Winnicott emphasized the idea of illusion[6] (1971a) as a positive experience, which he believes underlies the creation of intersubjective meanings that are neither external or purely internal (personal). Winnnicott (1960) illustrates the illusory, intersubjective, paradoxical aspects of meaning with the often quoted comment: "that there is no such thing as a baby." In this statement, Winnicott differentiates the baby as a biological entity from the baby as a center of psychological experience. Psychologically the baby only comes into existence within the context of the joint fantasies and emotional experiences that join mother and baby into a new, unique intersubjective unit. Winnicott elaborated this intersubjective process, the joint creation of meaning through illusion and fantasy,[7] in his development of the concept of transitional objects (the thumb, teddy bear, or blanket) which developed into the individual's capacity to have complex transitional experiences, intersubjective schemas, such as religion, art, families, and love affairs. For Winnicott the development of transitional experience involves the movement from the concrete thought of the paranoid schizoid to the symbolic thought of the depressive position.

Winnicott (1971a) describes the process of thinking somewhat differently than Bion and other Kleinians, explicitly differentiating thinking as occurring in two parallel realms, simultaneously in an objective realm of things where people are objects and a subjective realm in which people become centers of initiative, feelings, thoughts, and intentions. For Winnicott we live as both objects and subjects, differentiating our being in the external world of things and work from the intersubjective world of affect, meanings, and intimate relationships. Winnicott's view that we are potentially both subjects and objects[8] is similar to Buber's (1970) description of two modes of being in the world, a subjective experience which he describes as "I - Thou" and an experience of self and other as objects, in "I - It" forms of living. Although the difference between being an object and being a subject is implicit in other object relations theories, in making these two experiential realms of experience explicit, Winnicott presents a theory with which to understand the many patients who function extremely well in the objective world of things, business, law, and other professions, while simultaneously unable to be present in and know intersubjective aspect of life, including their own and others' feelings, inner worlds, intentions, desires and experiences. Grotstein (2000) describes individuals who primarily live in the world of objects and are unable to enter into intersubjective transitional experience involving self-awareness, art, intimate relationships, etc., as "orphans of the real."

Matte-Blanco (1988), a Chilean analyst who studied with Klein, conceptualized the mind differently from the traditional hierarchical structural approach. Rather than focusing on either anatomy or mechanics as models for the mind, he thought about the function of conscious and unconscious mentation and developed a dual theory in which conscious and unconscious thought reflected different functions. Conscious thought functioned as a means to know the external world of things and objects, and unconscious thought functioned to know the internal world of affects and subjective meaning. Like Winnicott, he separated thinking about the external world of objects from the internal world of subjective experience. Matte-Blanco suggested that consciousness, knowing the external world of objects, utilized asymmetrical logic which differentiated experience in terms of person, place, time, and causality, while unconscious experience is organized and generated by symmetrical logic, which identifies and creates similarities, dedifferentiating experience in terms of person, place, time, and causality, as in dreams which collapse these dimensions into a surrealist world of images. Langer (1942), a philosopher and linguist, similarly suggested two modes of symbolizing, knowing and articulating experience, which she described as discursive and presentational symbols. Discursive symbols translate experience from one mode to another as when we explain experience in terms of history or biology, or turn to universal principles and precedents, like the Oedipus complex, to understand a patient's difficulty with authority. Presentational symbols do not try to explain events but rather attempt to recreate the affective experience of an event, through identification, or creating dramatic or artistic experiences. For example, Hamlet brings us into a different emotional experience in experiencing our struggles with authority than does a discursive explanation of Oedipal or political dynamics. Discursive symbols, like asymmetrical logic, differentiate experience in terms of time, person, place, and causality while presentational symbols, like symmetrical logic, collapse differences within these dimensions and create an emotional experience as if we were involved in the experience. Picasso's painting of Guernica uses a symmetrical, presentational, surrealist mode to represent and evoke an experience of war, death, and destruction, while a newspaper article or history of the Spanish Civil War presents the same experience from an asymmetrical, discursive perspective. Again, both represent truth, the former the emotional, subjective truth and the later, the historical, causal, positivist truth of this war.

Symmetry and asymmetry are alternate, parallel modes of creating meaning and structuring interpretations in psychoanalysis and psychotherapy. Depending on which form of logic we use, the same experience may have different meanings and are understood differently in different realms of experience. Matte-Blanco (1988) suggests that when unbearable internal experiences are externalized through pathological projective identification and are not contained or elaborated by another person (parent or therapist) they become experienced asymmetrically as external experiences: concrete, immutable facts in the external world which cannot be altered. Bion's concepts of alpha function, reverie, and dream work can be understood as symmetrical processes of affective and symbolic elaboration in which the therapist's identifications and experiences of similarities are a first step in containing and elaborating a patient's dissociated, unconscious, concrete experience. We can think of this process of containment as a critical part of the interpretive process in which a therapist can use either an asymmetrical strategy attempting to differentiate time, person, place, and causality or a symmetrical strategy in which these differences are collapsed, creating poetic-like experiences of similarities and metaphors which provide an intense affective, presentational experience. For example, a therapist who believes that he/she is being experienced as a mother in the transference may say, using an asymmetrical strategy, "I am not your mother" attempting to help separate the patient from the repetition of past expectations and failed behaviors. Alternatively, using a symmetrical strategy the therapist may say, "I am your mother" highlighting the current emotional reality of the transference countertransference experience. Both statements are true; however, they each result in different affective and cognitive experiences for the patient and therapist. The asymmetrical strategy encourages a differentiation of the therapist from the historical object while the symmetrical strategy encourages the articulation of the affective experience of being a child in a nurturing relationship.

The following diagram presents in schematic form a two dimensional psychoanalytic theory of thinking (Newirth, 2003) which combines the concepts of the paranoid schizoid and depressive modes of thought with the dimensions of asymmetry and symmetry. This matrix presents the concrete thought of the paranoid schizoid position as both internal (symmetrical) and external (asymmetrical) experiences, contrasting the intense affective experiences of persecutory anxiety, terror, and nightmares with the frustrating experiences of obsessional states, literal responses, and the slicing of reality into smaller and smaller segments. The symbolic experiences within the depressive position contrast the symmetrical experiences such as the transcendent states of love, merger, and poetic language with asymmetrical experiences of abstract thought, historic and genetic explanations, and the law which regulates our behavior in the external world. The different experiences described in the Matrix of Mental Experience are meant as illustrations and not as an exhaustive list.

Table 2.1. The Matrix of Mental Experience

	Symmetry	*Asymmetry*
The paranoid-schizoid position: concrete thought processes	1. Body symptoms	1. Obsessional states
	2. Nightmares	2. Collection of details
	3. Persecutory anxiety	3. Literal responses
	4. States of terror	4. Fragmentation anxiety
	5. Falling through space	5. Splitting or slicing reality
The depressive position: symbolic thought processes	1. Dreams and creative fantasies	1. Abstract thought
	2. Empathy	2. Inferential process
	3. Poetry	3. Discursive writing
	4. Dedifferentiation of self and other	4. Genetic, transference interpretation
	5. Transcendence and ecstatic experience	5. The law
	6. Synchronic time	6. Diachronic time

DEVELOPMENTAL PSYCHOLOGY

Contemporary developmental psychology has an intersubjective focus on how people in the environment, typically parents, affect the developing infant's capacity to regulate emotions, represent and reflect on experience, and form relationships. Bowlby's (1969) work on attachment theory and the concept of working models provided a structural perspective, which describes the evolving relationship schemas reflecting the persistence of early attachment experiences. Beebe's (2005) study of moment to moment interaction between parent and infant presents in microscopic detail the process of mutual regulation, including the down regulation of affects, such as calming and withdrawal, and the up regulation of affects, in experiences of mutual pleasure, laughing, and anger. Stern's (1985) work on the psychological birth of the human infant brought into the foreground the intersubjective development of internal representation of self and other in the development of intersubjective relationship structures. Stern (1992) connected psychoanalytic concepts of unconscious fantasy (phantasy) with the development of the capacity to transform experience into thought, integrating contemporary cognitive and developmental findings into the concept of "pre-narrative envelopes," thought structures which emerge from the infant's intersubjective interactions and ongoing motivational states. Stern describes the pre-narrative envelope as the building blocks of thought which synthesize the flood of internal and external sensations and perception that the infant experiences from moment to moment. Although Stern does not connect his concept of pre-narrative envelopes with Kleinian concepts of splitting, projective identification, and symbolization, both theories suggest how early intersubjective experiences become integrated into more complex thought processes. Stern (1992) states:

> the mind appears to process, in parallel and in partial independence, a large number of simultaneous mental happenings. During an experience, instinctual urgings, visual images, affect shifts, sensations, motor actions, ideas, states of arousal, language, place and space, time, etc., are all processed simultaneously in parallel throughout all "centres" in the mind as well as in specialized ones devoted to processing each ("Parallel Distributed Processing" [PDP]). The parallel processing of each element is carried out with lower-level, local, mental operations which are never translatable into subjective experience. These mental processes are operationally unconscious. This results in a sort of mental pandemonium of mental action in multiple "centres" ("modules"): many characters in search of an author. This is the normal state of things. And from the interplay, co-ordination, integration of these lower-level processes, a more global mental event emerges: "an emergent property" of the mind, which has coherence and sense in the context in which it emerged. That is to say, the diverse events and feelings are tied together as necessary elements of a single unified happening which assumes a narrative-like structure. The "pre-narrative envelope" is just such an emergent property of mind that accomplishes this integration of experience. (p. 295)

Stern believes that these early processes of creating meaning, mental construction, or thinking utilize the infant's hard-wired capacity for pattern recognition, generalization, coherence, awareness of intentionality, and temporality which create schemas that organize the infant's action. Although not verbal, pre-narrative envelopes are organized around early experiences involving dramatic lines: plots which unfold along a temporal line. Stern (1992, p. 314) states that the pre-narrative envelope is: "the unit of experience from which later true autobiographical narrative acts of meaning are created. In this sense, it implies a discoverable order between the two, and views the hermeneutic approach as complimentary. From a clinical point of view, thinking in terms of 'pre-narrative envelopes' provides an additional search strategy for the origins of the patient's representational world. It puts a greater emphasis on the detailed exploration of repeated 'micro-interactions' in both past and present."

Stern and his colleagues (1998) applied developmental, cognitive, and nonlinear dynamic systems theory to the process of change in psychoanalysis and psychotherapy. They began by highlighting the idea that something more than interpretation brings about change and growth in psychotherapy. They (Stern et al., 1998 p. 903) "suggest something more," like the infant's development of pre-narrative envelopes or the Kleinian concept of unconscious fantasy, occurs in the nonverbal realm of intersubjective interactions between therapist and patient which they define as "implicit relational knowing" which is distinct from symbolic[9] knowledge developed through verbal interpretation and explicit knowledge. Stern et al. (1998, p. 904) cite the cognitive and developmental literature in a view of the mind that involves two parallel organizations which each function according to different psychological processes including:

> At least two kinds of knowledge, two kinds of representations, and two kinds of memory are constructed and re-organized in dynamic psychotherapies. One is explicit (declarative) and the other is implicit (procedural). Whether they are in fact two distinct mental phenomena remains to be determined. At this stage, however, we believe that further enquiry demands that they be considered separately . . . declarative knowledge is gained or acquired through verbal interpretations that alter the patient's intrapsychic understanding within the context of (interpreting) the "psychoanalytic," and usually transferential, relationship. Implicit relational knowing, on the other hand, occurs through "interactional, intersubjective processes" that alter the relational field within the context of what we will call the "shared implicit relationship." (p. 904)

In elaborating their argument, these authors point out that anecdotal accounts of successful psychotherapy suggest that patients remember two kinds of experiences: the first involves interpretations that rearranged their conscious narrative while the second involved special "moments" of emotionally heightened connection between patient and therapist which alter his/her sense of self and the implicit procedural relational knowing which had up until that point structured their relationship, their way of being with others. These authors emphasize that from infancy onward we develop schemas of nonverbal, implicit, procedural knowledge of how to be with others; narrative structures or scripts which define how we enter into and nonverbally instruct others how to be with us.

Unlike many psychoanalytically informed authors who also describe the mother-infant experience as a model for psychoanalysis and psychotherapy, these authors (Stern et al., 1998; BCPSG, 2007) emphasize a temporal gradient, suggesting that intersubjective relationships are not static but are constantly moving forward, motivated, following an intentional plan, a direction. They focus on time as a central aspect of experience, describing the therapy relationship as "moving along." However, this is not a simple linear model of time with equal units such as minutes, hours, and days, but a two dimensional concept of time, which includes a horizontal axis of diachronic time (minutes, hours, days, etc.) and a vertical axis of synchronic time which includes both repetitive experiences of relationships (for example with women or authority figures), and a dimension of intensity, special moments that occur in the intersubjective field which demand an immediate response and can alter the course of the relationship and the paradigm for implicit relation knowing. They describe this movement through time as consisting of a regular flow of prosaic experience, "moving along," which we might think of as similar to engaging in regular conversations, something like Buber's concept of "I - It" experience, and "moments of meeting," in which the greater emotional intensity and presence of the participants can be compared to Buber's concept of "I - Thou" relatedness, and a further state of intensity within moments of meeting, "now moments," moments of greater emotional intensity which demand a shift from the usual forms of relatedness to something new, often emotionally challenging to both participants' self perceptions, such as when a patient suddenly asks a difficult question, such as "do you love me." Stern et al. (1998) suggest that

> the (now) "moment" takes on cardinal importance as the basic unit of subjective change in the domain of "implicit relational knowing." When a change occurs in the intersubjective environment, a "moment of meeting" will have precipitated it. The change will be sensed and the newly altered environment then acts as the new effective context in which subsequent mental actions occur and are shaped and past events are reorganized. The relationship as implicitly known has been altered, thus changing mental actions and behaviors that assemble in this different context. (p. 906)

In developing the concept of implicit relational knowing, the Boston Change Process Study Group[10] (BCPSG, 2007) contrasts this concept with many one-person, hierarchical concepts of classical psychoanalysis and ego psychology. They suggest that their emphasis on the implicit realm as contrasted with the explicit realm does not represent a simple version of nonverbal as contrasted with verbal knowing, or between infantile and adult experience. Implicit relational knowing highlights a model of the mind which does not privilege verbal consciousness, recognizing that much knowledge and behavior is organized outside of consciousness, including what has been referred to as procedural learning. Implicit relational knowing involves two dimensions, a nonverbal process of creating meaning, like the pre-narrative envelopes, which organize relational patterns of being with and expectations for others, and an expanded use of the concept of procedural learning (Nahum, 2008). Nahum (2008) discusses the use of procedural learning as a way of explaining one dimension of implicit relational knowing. Traditionally procedural learning has described complex learning between people and things in the physical world such as learning to ride a bicycle. Nahum (2008) suggests that the complex world of intersubjective relationships involves procedural learning of greater complexity and importance than learning to ride a bicycle. In a recent paper I (see chapter 8) suggested that implicit procedural learning is critical in many intersubjective relationships such as the psychoanalytic supervisory relationship, as well as learning to flirt and be in other complex intersubjective relationships. In important intersubjective relationships verbal, asymmetrical instructions fall short. They fail because complex intersubjective relatedness requires experiences of trust that the other person will not let you down, and confidence that: "I will not be shamed"; perhaps, like learning to ride a bicycle, implicit relational learning also requires a willingness to fall on one's face while gaining experience.

The Boston Change Process Study Group (BCPSG, 2007) illustrates the nonverbal development of implicit procedural learning citing attachment studies which show that early patterns of implicit procedural learning develop by 12 months of age as "forms of parent-child affective dialogue over the first year of life, including parental suppressed anger and discomfort with close physical contact (Main, Tomasini, & Tolan, 1979) and parental mock-surprise expressions to infant anger (Malatesta et al., 1989). Such restrictions in the parent-child affective dialogue are foreshadowed by the parent's style of discussing attachment experiences in interviews prior to the child's birth and they remain evident in the parent's organization of thinking about attachment-related topics long after infancy." Attachment research provides a great deal of support for the concept of implicit relational knowing and the importance of the intersubjective relationship between patient and therapist.

Fonagy and his associates (2003) developed a model of the mind which is inherently social, focusing on the intersubjective experience between the child and parents within the context of attachment theory. They (Fonagy, 2000; Fonagy et al., 2003) describe the importance of secure attachment as the intersubjective matrix which allows for development of "mentalization," the capacity to know one's own and an other's mind, including the ability to reflect on thought process and be aware of one's and the other's intentionality. Fonagy (2000, p. 1129) suggests that individuals who experience early trauma may not develop the capacity to mentalize as a way "to avoid having to think about their caregiver's wish to harm them." Although he bases his discussion on attachment and developmental research, Fonagy's discussion of the development of the capacity for mentalization is quite similar to Kleininan concepts of symbolization within the depressive position; both require a capacity for emotional separateness, a view of possibility, and the capacity to reflect on the content of one's own and another's mind. Fonagy et al. (2003) contextualize the capacity for mentalization or symbolization within the evolution of attachment experiences and state that:

> a major selective advantage conferred by attachment to humans is the opportunity it afforded for the development of social intelligence and meaning making: attachment actually propels cognitive development. The capacity for "interpretation," which Bogdan (1997) defined as "organisms making sense of each other in contexts where this matters biologically" (p. 10), becomes uniquely human when others are engaged "psychologically in sharing experiences, information and affects" (p. 94). The capacity to interpret human behavior—to make sense of each other—requires the intentional stance: "treating the object whose behavior you want to predict as a rational agent with beliefs and desires" (Dennett, 1987, p. 15). (p. 415)

Fonagy's concept of mentalization is different from previous theories of thinking in that he describes the development of the capacity for mentalization as the result of integrating two earlier and more basic forms of thought (Fonagy and Target, 1996; Target and Fonagy, 1996): psychic equivalence and the pretend mode. Although these two modes of thought are described as originally occurring during infancy, versions of these thought patterns continue throughout life. In the mode of psychic equivalence (Fonagy and Target, 1969) the child (person) "equates the internal with the external. What exists in the mind must exist in the external world, and what exists out there must invariably also exist in the mind. There cannot be differences in perspective about the external world because it is isomorphic with the internal." Fonagy's mode of psychic equivalence is similar to Segal's (1950) concept of concrete thought in the paranoid schizoid position and provides a perspective on projective identification, suggesting that when something is projected or externalized it is experienced as a real event in the external world; that is, if I project my angry feelings into you I experience it as a fact, as reality. In the pretend mode (Fonagy and Target, 1969; 2007) thoughts are decoupled from external (physical) reality and are experienced as not connected to the external world, a kind of safe place, a psychic retreat. In describing the pretend mode, Fonagy and his associates are describing a means of experiencing and creating knowledge, of testing and expanding meaning through imagination. Like Winnicott's discussion of the importance of paradox and illusion, Fonagy sees this mode of thought as being fragile and easily disrupted and undermined if an adult questions a child's play. Fonagy and Target (2007, p. 928) illustrate the fragility of the pretend mode with the following example: "a boy, aged 2 1/2 years, was playing that an upside-down chair was a tank with the legs shooting ammunition, his father asked him, 'Is this a chair or a tank?' The little boy stopped playing, put the chair the right way up and walked away. He knew that the object was a chair and not a tank, but in the pretend mode bringing external reality into contact with the play destroys the possibility of imagination." How different the child's experience would have been if his father had joined him in playing war.

As we see in this example, play can exist as a singular activity of the child in which aspects of experience become integrated and expressed, perhaps in this last example as experimenting with healthy oedipal aggression, or it may become dissociated as a form of psychic retreat. In constructive development the child develops the capacity to pretend with friends and family, introducing the possibility for the child of the creation of an intersubjective reality, like Winnicott's concept of transitional experience. For Fonagy and Target (2007, p. 928) the development of intersubjective play in the pretend mode is highly significant: "for once, the power to make reality lies more in one's own mind; but it also becomes real through being shared." These intersubjective experiences of mutual play (pretend) occur between parents and children in secure attachment relationships where the parents often take on the important role of mirroring the child's experience and affect.

Fonagy, as is true of other developmental psychologists, is very specific about the process of mirroring, an intersubjective experience in which the parent re-presents the child's affect or experience in an exaggerated form, thereby marking it as a mental state rather than an external event. If the parent is unable to experience the child's affect as a mental state, but rather becomes flooded by the affect itself, as if it is real, then the child will experience it within the mode of psychic equivalence as real and reflecting the parent's and not the child's experience. For mirroring to be successful it needs to be marked, an exaggerated presentation of affect and action. Fonagy et al.'s concept of mirroring seems to be describing the use of presentational, symmetrical symbols and language and not discursive, asymmetrical symbols and language. Descriptions of mirroring as marked intersubjective experiences suggests an interesting perspective on failures of projective identification where the parent becomes frightened by the child's angry or fearful projections and is unable to provide an experience of containment, reverie, and symbolization and the child is left to re-internalize a sense of badness in the mode of psychic equivalence while experiencing the parent as critical and angry.

Mentalization is an emergent quality of mind in which the pretend mode and the mode of psychic equivalence become integrated, reflecting the child's and adult's interest in his/her own and the other's mind. This interest in minds, in mental processes including affect, intention, and memory involves the experience of the self and others as agents who act purposefully and can be understood through the recall of past interactions. In the safety of a relationship the child can discover that what is in his/her mind is not necessarily in the other's mind through a process of testing in which each participant is able to observe the other's reaction and infer a mental process. Fonagy et al.'s (2003, p. 929) description of the child's experience of loss in developing the capacity for mentalization echoes many aspects of the depressive position as well as Lacan's (1996) concept of the symbolic order:

> With the arrival of mentalization, the child suddenly recognizes that he cannot be sure what the minds within other bodies think or feel. Physical reality does not specify the other's state of mind, what he knows is not the limit of knowledge of minds, and simply thinking something does not make it true. This recognition entails a sense of loss, including loss of control over the external world, but it also gives him a precious new tool for understanding the actions of others for which previously only crude interpretations in terms of physical constraints and observable goals could be given (teleological thinking) (Gergely & Csibra, 1996, 1997, 2003; Csibra & Gergely, 1998).

Fonagy and his associates (Fonagy et al., 2003; Fonagy & Target, 2007) believe that failure in the development of the capacity for mentalization coincides with important aspects of psychopathology particularly for patients described as representing borderline personality disorders. For such people their sense of disorganized attachment makes relationships highly problematic. This is often amplified by their inability to control and know what is in others' minds, because of an over dependence on the mode of psychic equivalence resulting in the belief that what is in their mind is a fact, and the inability to enter the pretend mode with others but rather to be isolated in the retreat to their own imaginative elaborations of experience. All of these difficulties are well known to clinicians and following this developmental argument shed light on persistent and difficult problems including the clinician's inability to mirror in a marked way the patient's experience.

COGNITIVE AND NEUROPSYCHOLOGY

Many psychoanalysts have become interested in the convergence of contemporary psychoanalytic ideas about the construction of meaning, and developments in cognitive psychology and neuropsychology. Memory, affects, and the ability to reconstruct past events as they influence present behavior, have all been at the core of psychoanalytic thinking. Cortina and Liotti (2007) describe two separate cognitive modes, parallel forms of memory, thought, and information processing: the implicit/procedural and the explicit/declarative memory system. The amygdala (Mancia, 2006) is a central neuropsychological structure integrating affective experience and the implicit/procedural memory system which organizes emotional and intersubjective experience in infancy and continues through life. The implicit/procedural system processes information from early infancy continuing into childhood, and is the system that integrates multiple affective, sensory, and perceptual experiences which are not dependent on verbal ability. Procedural learning (and memory) involves complex sensorimotor experience such as learning to play instruments and sports, as well as complex intersubjective affective relationships. Procedural learning has typically discussed in relation to complex physical activities that require the ability to rapidly respond to multiple channels of feedback such as learning to ride a bicycle. However, as Stern (2004) and Newirth (chapter 8) have pointed out, complex intersubjective tasks dominate the psychological landscape—including: asking for help, flirting, being in love, learning psychoanalysis—require the capacity to rapidly respond to frequent, nonverbal feedback, in intersubjective goal directed activities. Like learning to ride a bicycle these intersubjective activities also require the presence of trust and the willingness to take risks, and returning to the bicycle metaphor, a willingness to fall on your face and not be crippled by shame.

Tulving (1972) introduced an important distinction within the explicit/declarative memory system describing two subsystems: semantic and episodic memory. Semantic memory involves general, atemporal, storage of information while the episodic memory involves autobiographical information, personal events, such as a memory of a birthday party or a parental disappointment. As more events are experienced, these memories become generalized and form prototypical stories, scripts which define sequences and expectations which organize and direct future behaviors. The development of scripts (Cortina and Liotti, 2007) allows events to be seen from multiple perspectives (depressive position) and the opportunity to develop verbal explanations which link past, present, and future in autobiographical memories that are accessible to conscious thought. Both forms of explicit/declarative memories are capable of becoming conscious and verbalized, utilizing asymmetrical logic, differentiating time, person, place, and causality. Lichtenberg, Lachmann, and Fossage (1992) adapted the idea of cognitive scripts, and describe patients' model scenes, narratives in which the person becomes a protagonist reliving the same relationship dynamics in new, repeating situations. Brunner (cited in Cortina and Liotti, 2007) suggests that the capacity to narrate experience is the "single most important way in which humans create meaning" which has also been a central theme in many revisions of psychoanalytic theory (Shafer, 1976; Hoffman, 2014).

The implicit and explicit memory systems function in parallel to each other, processing experience from different, simultaneous perspectives. Cortina and Liotti (2007) illustrate the parallel, interactive functions of the implicit/procedural and explicit/declarative memory systems through a discussion of the neurological condition of Korsakoff syndrome.

> In this syndrome, there is bilateral damage to parts of the temporal lobe and hippocampus. The main function of the hippocampus is to consolidate experience learned at an implicit/procedural level into long-term, explicit/declarative memory. Patients with this syndrome have complete amnesia of having met a person just a few minutes or hours after their encounter. This is because the capacity to encode and consolidate memories in long-term memory is destroyed by the lesions. Yet implicit/procedural memories are still present. For instance, depending on whether a person in a recent interaction was kind or mean, patients with this syndrome will, a few days or weeks later, have a strong positive or negative emotional response based on this experience, yet will be unable to account for these preferences (Damasio, 1999). Implicit memory is best modeled in terms of a massive parallel distributive process that involves all perceptual modalities and contains a massive amount of information. Due to the destruction of the hippocampus, this massive implicit learning system cannot be consolidated into the explicit and declarative memory system. Long-term memory stored before the lesion, memory that is widely distributed throughout the neocortex, remains intact. Hence these patients have excellent long-term memories. A certain degree of dissociation between the implicit and explicit systems is normal as long as there is a smooth transition from the experience encoded in these two memory systems and there are no striking contradictions between them. (p. 207)

Korsakoff syndrome illustrates the development of psychological and neurological understanding in terms of the parallel and separate functions of the implicit/procedural and explicit/declarative memory systems. This development of knowledge is a result of the increasing availability of new technologies such as the fMRI and other techniques which have allowed for the localization of different memory, motor, and language functions. One of the emerging aspects of this growth in knowledge is the awareness of the social brain, a growing awareness that we are hard wired for intersubjective emotional relationships, attachment, and language experiences. One interesting finding in this area has been the discovery of mirror neurons. Wolf et al. (2001, p. 94) describe mirror neurons as visual/motor neurons, multimodal neurons (Graziano and Gross, 1994) that can be activated simultaneously by different sensory modalities, including: auditory, somatosensory, and visual. These authors suggest that while multimodal neurons are present throughout the brain, it is of particular interest that they demonstrate plasticity in the amygdala, a limbic structure believed to enhance emotional memory. The mirror neurons are located in an area that is associated with speech but function like a motor neuron, firing when the subject acts, and like a sensory neuron, firing when the subject perceives another's actions. These neurons can be thought of as a biological analog for empathy, a neurological experience as one person observes another's activity and responds emotionally as if the person him or herself had been doing the observed action. We have all had this type of emotional experience with another person, when we observe a baby or someone experiencing intense pain or joy. Other neuropsychological observations show areas of the brain related to pain are activated when an affectively concerned person witnesses a suffering subject as well as in response to verbal communication. Rizzolatti and Arbib (1998, p. 188) (as cited in Wolf et al., 2001) suggest "that mirror neurons have the capacity to represent actions and, hence, ultimately "represent the link between sender and receiver" through which primitive, nonverbal, implicit communication begins.

Mancia (2006) suggests that mirror neurons may underlie processes of projective identification and suggests that the analyst attending to his/her countertransference experiences can provide an intersubjective affective, implicit experience through which both analyst and patient may experience the same feelings and implicit meanings. He also (Mancia, 2008) suggests that the unconscious nucleus of the self, stored in implicit memory, functions according to Matte-Blanco's concept of symmetrical logic and is:

> dominated by the symmetric, homogenizing and infinitizing way of being, and therefore acquires a logic that places it outside time and space. It therefore tends toward absolute symmetry . . . In this it differs from the repressed unconscious, formed later after the development of the declarative, explicit memory, which, according to Matte-Blanco, has an asymmetric logic. (p. 208)

Schore (2011, 2009a, 2009b) cites a great deal of neuropsychological evidence which differentiates the functions of the right and left brain hemispheres. The left hemisphere is specialized in sequential logic and represents conscious, explicit memory associated with processes described by Matte-Blanco (1998) as asymmetrical logic. The right hemisphere seems to organize experience around affect and implicit processes such as procedural learning, pattern recognition and similarity which were described by Matte-Blanco as symmetrical logic. Schore (2011) locates the early forming implicit self in the right hemisphere in contrast to the explicit, verbal, conscious self located in the left hemisphere. This differentiation of the implicit and explicit self is similar to developmental psychologists' observation that early implicit memories are organized through the functioning of the amygdala while later forming explicit memories are integrated through the functioning of the hippocampus. The developing right brain (Schore 2011, p. 80) is social or more specifically intersubjective and critically affected and dependent on early attachment experiences in which:

> implicit affective attachment interactions directly impact the experience dependent maturation of the right hemisphere (Ammaniti & Trentini, 2009; Schore, 1994, 2003a, 2003b, 2009a, 2009b; Siegel, 1999). The highest centers of this hemisphere, especially the orbitofrontal cortex, the locus of Bowlby's attachment system, act as the brain's most complex affect and stress regulatory

system (Cerqueira, Almeida, & Sousa, 2008; Schore, 1994, 2000) . . . Neuroscientists now contend that throughout the lifespan, the neural substrates of the perception of voices, faces, gestures, smells and pheromones, as evidenced by modern neuroimaging techniques, are characterized by a general pattern of right hemispheric functional asymmetry" (Brancucci, Lucci, Mazzatenta, & Tommasi, 2009, p. 895). (p. 80)

Schore (2011, p. 81) suggests that the failure of adequately attuned functioning leaves patients "susceptible to mind–body metabolic collapse, and thereby a loss of energy-dependent synaptic connectivity within the right brain, expressed in a sudden implosion of the implicit self, a rupture of self-continuity, and a loss of an ability to experience conscious affect. This collapse of the implicit self is signaled by the amplification of the effects of shame and disgust, and by the cognitions of hopelessness and helplessness. Because the right hemisphere mediates the communication and regulation of emotional states, the rupture of intersubjectivity is accompanied by an instant dissipation of safety and trust, a common occurrence in the treatment of the right brain deficits of the severe personality disorders (Schore, 2007; 2009b)."

In presenting a neuropsychological perspective on disorders of the right hemisphere Schore (2011) highlights the difference between functioning in the external world of things and the intersubjectivity of intimate, personal relationships. This difference is important in understanding psychotherapy and psychoanalysis where difficulties in right brain affective relationships dominate. Schore (2011) emphasizes the importance of the implicit intersubjective processes and communication in psychotherapy and psychoanalysis which he describes as "right brain to right brain" communication that he connects with now moments (Stern et al., 1998), enactments (BCPSG, 2007), and processes of intuition. Intuition, like other types of implicit procedural learning, is an experience near term which we immediately understand but is hard to define and teach. "Narvaez (2010) (cited in Schore, 2011) noted that individuals who access 'experience-based, postreflective, well-educated intuition' behave differently, that is 'they know what action would be effective and how to carry it out. Moreover, they have 'negative expertise'—they know what actions not to take in solving a problem and pay attention to intuitions that signal uncertainty' (p. 171). Citing a large body of research she concluded that whereas novices use conscious, effortful methods to solve problems, the well-educated intuition of experts incorporates 'far more sophisticated unconscious deep and automatic knowledge that may have been painfully learned' (p. 171)."

Stern (2004) proposed that the clinician focus attention on brief moments and intuitively grasp the relational and emotional essence of that present moment, without it being verbalized. Other clinicians have hypothesized that the intuition of an experienced expert therapist lies fundamentally in a process of unconscious pattern matching (Rosenblatt & Thickstun, 1994) and that this pattern recognition follows a nonverbal path, as verbal activity interferes with achieving insight (Schooler & Melcher, 1995). Bucci (1997) developed a transformational model of representational activity (RA) in which she describes the transformation of sub-symbolic, implicit experience and mentation into symbolic, explicit experience and mentation. She has been able to identify the movement from implicit experience to symbolic or narrative experience in her studies of the psychoanalytic process, where this movement often indicates a change in the patient's affective experience. Schore (2011) focusing on the intuitive, transformational aspects of psychoanalysis and psychotherapy and cites the following authors:

> Welling (2005) offered a phase model, in which the amount of information contained in the intuition increases from one phase to another, resulting in increased levels of complexity. An early "detection phase" related to "functions of arousal and attention" culminates in a "metaphorical solution phase," in which the intuition presents itself in the form of kinesthetic sensations, feelings, images, metaphors, and words. Here the solution, which has an emotional quality, is revealed, but in a veiled nonverbal form. Thes descriptions reflect the activity of the right hemisphere, which is dominant for attention (Raz, 2004), kinesthesia (Naito et al., 2005), unique modes of perception associated with mental creativity (Asari et al., 2008), and the processing of novel metaphors (Mashal, Faust, Hendler, & Jung-Beeman, 2007). In contrast to the left brain's deliberate, conscious, analytical search strategies, the right brain generates the subjective experience of insight, whereby a novel solution is computed unconsciously and subsequently emerges into awareness suddenly (Bowden & Jung Beeman, 1998; Kounios & Beeman, 2009; Sandkuhler & Bhattacharya, 2008). (p. 92)

CONCLUDING COMMENTS AND DESCRIPTION OF THE CHART: CONVERGING MODELS OF THE MIND

This chapter has presented converging conceptual developments in the separate areas of contemporary psychoanalytic theory, developmental psychology, cognitive psychology and neuropsychology. In each of these areas the mind has been reconceptualized as an intersubjective, nonhierarchical, multidimensional and interactive structure which is dependent on social experience; has a dual, parallel system of encoding memories and processing information differently when the source is located in the emotional world as opposed to the world of things; mental representations precede and are separate from verbal representations and language; having the capacity to continue to change and grow. The following table presents these ideas in relation to the dual conceptual structures understood as processing information separately in the external world and the internal world. The third column presents some ideas on the intersubjective level of mental experience, that is those aspects of thought which develop between people. This table also provides a means of connecting the terms that have been used in the different academic disciplines through which we can connect similar and overlapping concepts. In the following chapters we expand on this model of the mind and the use of symmetrical, presentational interventions in the development of the implicit/procedural domain of clinical work.

Table 2.2. Converging Approaches to the Mind

Approach	*Theorist*	*External World*	*Internal World*	*Intersubjective Process*
Psychoanalytic Theory	Klein	Paranoid Schizoid – Concrete thought	Depressive – Symbolic thought	Projective identification
	Segal	Symbolic equivalents	True symbols	
	Bion	Beta elements	Alpha Function Container – contained Waking dream	Reverie
	Winnicott	Object	Subject	Transitional experience
	Matte-Blanco	Asymmetrical logic	Symmetrical logic	
Linguistic / Philosophical	S. Langer	Discursive symbols	Presentational symbols	
	M. Buber	I – It	I – Thou	
Developmental	Fonagy	Mode of psychic equivalents	Mode of Play	Mentalization / Reflective Function
	Bebee	Symbolic representations	Presymbolic representations	Mutual regulation of affect
	BPCSG	Declarative verbal domain Moving along	Implicit procedural domain Present moments / now moments	Shared implicit relationship
	Stern		Pre-Narrative Envelopes (RIGS)	
Cognitive	Bucci	Subsymbolic Working memory Explicit / Declarative memory Semantic memory Episodic memory	Symbolic Long term memory Implicit / Procedural memory Procedural learning Emotional memory Autobiographical memory	Referential activity Emotional schemas
Neuropsychological	Shore	Left Brain Hippocampus	Right Brain Amygdala	Mirror neurons

NOTES

1. I use the intersubjective rather than interpersonal or social to focus on the internal experience and intention rather than the observable action of each participant in an interaction.

2. Sullivan's similarly altered the locus of the mind from an internal to an interpersonal experience.

3. See Freud (1950) Project in which he attempted to see all mental activity as reflected in brain function.

4. This shift in perspective was similar to the shift in perspective from realism in art to expressionism and surrealism.

5. I am using "mother" because Bion assumes that the parent who was engaged in this process was the mother, when in fact it can be any committed caretaker including a father.

6. His use of the concept of illusion can be compared to the Kleinian concept of phantasy each of which emphasize an unconscious process which may be thought of as a surrealist as opposed to an objective experience.

7. I use the spelling of fantasy with an f, rather than ph, and will differentiate the function of fantasy thought elaborating the intra and intersubjective contexts of these experiences.

8. In earlier work Winnicott (1955) described this dual form of being and thinking as the true self and the false self. As Khan (1975) states these early ideas had a somewhat moralistic tone which the latter concept of object and subject did not have.

9. Stern and his colleagues use the term symbolic as a synonym for verbal. I disagree with that usage since Stern describes instances of nonverbal symbolic organizations such as the concept of pre-narrative envelopes. In my discussion of the work of Stern and his colleagues I will substitute verbal for symbolic in order to make it more consistent with other theories.

10. The Boston Change Process Study Group includes many of the authors who have worked with Stern for many years and continue to develop ideas around implicit procedural knowing.

Chapter Three

The Dream as a Transformational Experience

Cultural and Psychoanalytic Perspectives

INTRODUCTION

The Interpretation of Dreams

The publication of *The Interpretation of Dreams* (Freud, 1900) marks the origin of psychoanalysis as the study of dreams through which Freud described the relationship between unconscious processes and conscious experience. Freud's view of the hierarchical structure of the mind and the central importance of unconscious thought is expressed in the frequently quoted comment that the goal of psychoanalysis is making the unconscious conscious. In describing this process, Freud developed the method of free association and introduced interpretation as a process of translation in which the analyst and patient were able to understand the hidden meanings of dreams. Freud thought of dreams as the royal road to the unconscious. He developed a positivist, archeological approach to dreams, which, like hysteria, had previously been thought of as outside the realm of scientific inquiry (Szasz, 1974). The dream occupies a special place in psychoanalysis; it defined the qualities of unconscious thought, provided a method through which to uncover the hidden wishes that motivated behavior, and introduced the possibility of certainty in psychoanalytic knowledge. Unfortunately, Freud's archeological approach to dreams limited psychoanalysis's understanding of dreams and the function of unconscious thought to hidden, often infantile content and avoided personal truth.

Dreams in Culture, Art, Poetry, and Everyday Life

In culture, art, poetry, and everyday language, dreams encompass a broader set of meanings; they look to the future and not the past, they reflect our capacity for hope, opportunities to transcend the repetitiveness of our histories and the banal present; they often present the possibility of transforming ourselves and our world. The power of this transformational view of dreams is found in poetry, drama, song, and other cultural experiences in which new meanings are created which restructure our experience. Tevye's dream in *Fiddler on the Roof* and the song, "The Impossible Dream" from the play *Man of La Mancha* point to the transformational aspect of dreams through which we can change the direction and the emotional quality of our lives often moving from a sense of powerlessness and persecution, living in a paranoid state, to one of hopefulness, responsibility and agency as in the depressive position. Langston Hughes's (1995) poem "Dreams" suggests the importance of dreams as providing a sense of hope and aliveness.

Hold fast to dreams
For when dreams go
Life is a barren field
Frozen with snow.

Dr. Martin Luther King's speech, "I Have a Dream"[1] is an extraordinarily powerful illustration of the transformational nature of dreams as a cultural and symbolic experience. In his speech he uses the concept of a dream simultaneously as a metaphor and as an invitation to join him in a dream-like experience of social dreaming. Dr. King's speech engaged deep unconscious structures which metaphorically articulated the exploitation of Black people and provided both meaning and hope through the use of psychoanalytic and literary processes of condensation, displacement, rhythm, metaphor, emotional images, and the evocative, dramatic use of presentational language. Dr. King began by describing the history of injustice, the primary economic benefits that slavery provided to the country, the resulting poverty and persecution that Black Americans suffered during and after slavery, and then he distilled this historic experience, creating an extremely powerful and evocative economic metaphor, stating: "we were gathered in Washington DC to collect an overdue debt!" As he spoke, he moved from the economic metaphor of an "overdue debt" to a series of powerful poetic images in which through the use of symmetrical language he became the voice of disowned desires, effacing differences between himself and the audience, collapsing the dimensions of time, person, and place, and creating a possible dream in which hope and community replace hatred and prejudice.

As in a dream, Dr. King creates intense emotional and visual images through repetition and metaphor. He begins with the powerful image of living "on a lonely island of poverty in the midst of a vast ocean of material prosperity." He is not simply describing historical facts but his dream-like language generates an emotional experience. He then builds on this image and suggests that Black people have been presented with a check marked insufficient funds:

> In a sense we've come to our nation's capital to cash a check. When the architects of our republic wrote the magnificent words of the Constitution and the Declaration of Independence, they were signing a promissory note to which every American was to fall heir. This note was a promise that all men, yes, black men as well as white men, would be guaranteed the "unalienable Rights" of "Life, Liberty and the pursuit of Happiness." It is obvious today that America has defaulted on this promissory note, insofar as her citizens of color are concerned. Instead of honoring this sacred obligation, America has given the Negro people a bad check, a check which has come back marked "insufficient funds."
>
> But we refuse to believe that the bank of justice is bankrupt. We refuse to believe that there are insufficient funds in the great vaults of opportunity of this nation. And so, we've come to cash this check, a check that will give us upon demand the riches of freedom and the security of justice.

Dr. King understood dreams not simply as reflections of past experiences but as powerful transformational structures which allow us to imagine, experience, and articulate visions of the future: desires, hopes, and possibilities. In listening to his speech the members of the audience become subjects developing a new, powerful voice, rather than feeling silenced, the passive victims of history. Dr. King than develops two additional experiences, one of hope in a series of stanzas which begin with the phrase "I have a dream" and then he points to a future in which he locates development of the promise of freedom in the locations where it does not exist, through a stirring set of images, presentational symbols, beginning with the statement "Let Freedom Ring." Dr. King's use of the dream, as both a metaphor and as a transformational experience, reverses the traditional psychoanalytic strategy of making the unconscious conscious, his speech infuses new unconscious experiences of identification, hope, possibility, connection, and love into the bleak conscious experiences of the lives of Black Americans.

Dr. King was a master of speaking to the unconscious. His use of metaphors, and naturally speaking in the emotional language of the right brain, collapsing asymmetrical distinctions between person, place, time, and causality so that time exists only in the present. From the perspective of the BPCSG, we would say that he brings a sense of urgency short circuiting the process of moving through time. He defines the present moment as a "now" moment, one that could potentially change the direction of the ongoing problems of race in America. The speech has a sense of forward movement in time; we are not simply focused on the past as a series of impersonal historical events but are moving into the future, reflecting intentionality that is one of the core features of mentalization.

Dr. King understands the implicit structure of dreams as he repeats several powerful phrases: "I have a dream," and "let freedom ring." In dreams, poems, artistic and intimate experiences, images, words, and phrases are often repeated. Matte-Blanco discusses this phenomena of repetition as part of symmetrical logic suggesting that the emotional space of dreams has an infinite number of dimensions while external reality organized through asymmetrical logic has only three spatial and one temporal dimension, through which information about the external world is expressed. Repetition is the way that these infinite (N) dimensions of affective experience, including the intensity of the emotional experience, are both created and expressed as Dr. King's speech creates an intense affective experience through the repetition of phrases through which he also creates a hopeful future that may resolve the horror of the past.

The Dream as a Transformational Experience in Psychoanalysis

Contemporary psychoanalytic understanding of dreams has evolved a great deal since Freud's pioneering work. The dream is no longer seen as a depository of "hidden truths" which can be translated into understandable memories,[2] but as representing affective schemas, right brain structures, which define how a person organizes his/her relationships with self and others in the world. Fosshage and Lachman (Lichtenberg, Lachman, Fosshage, & Rotenberg, 1997) describe these schemas as model scenes while other theorists describe them as scripts through which we live out and repeat early relationship patterns as if they are our fate. Contemporary object relations theorists conceptualize the dream as a process, structure, or apparatus for processing sensory, emotional, and cognitive experiences into meaningful thought rather than thinking of it as primarily reflecting repressed wishes, bits of hidden or forgotten content.

Contemporary object relations theorists have extended Klein's (1946), Bion's (1962) and Winnicott's (1971a) concept of symbolism and the depressive position, viewing the dream as a process of transforming the concrete experiences of the paranoid schizoid position into the symbolic, meaningful, reflective thought processes of the depressive position. In separating the content of the dream and the process of creating dream thoughts they view therapy and psychoanalysis as a process through which the capacity to dream can be developed which allows the individual to transform sensory, affective, and cognitive experience into personally meaningful symbolic experience.

This transformational perspective extends Klein's (1946) concept of phantasy, Bion's (1965) concept of alpha function, and Winnicott's (1971a) concept of transitional experiences. Each of these concepts describes the transformation of the concrete experiences of the paranoid schizoid position into the symbolic experiences of the depressive position. Dreaming and reverie are thought of as developmental processes which increasingly are capable of generating subjective meanings; transforming passive, persecutory experiences into active, subjective, symbolic experiences. These theorists use different concepts which reflect nuances in understanding the dream as a transformational process. Bion's theories are a continuous attempt to work out this transformational model which he described in several ways: as alpha function, reverie, the container contained, and waking dream thoughts. Winnicott's (1971a) concept of transitional experience describes the development of the capacity to use symbolic thought from a less abstract and more romantic, phenomological perspective. Grotstein (1979), Ogden (2003, 2004a, 2004b), Ferro (2009), and Newirth (2003) have highlighted a shift in the psychoanalytic understanding of dreams from simply a source of hidden or disguised meaning to a transformational process that generates new meanings, hope, and the affective experiences of being fully alive. These authors emphasized that this contemporary object relations approach to dreams involves a focus on developing the capacity to creating meaning rather than on dream content.

Ogden (2003, 2004a, 2004b) elaborates Bion's concept of dreaming as a developing capacity to link concrete, fragmented, sensory experiences and internal affective states so that they become meaningful emotional experiences. For Ogden (2003, p. 18), dreaming is the "work of making unconscious linkages—as opposed to forms of psychic evacuation, such as hallucination, excessive projective identification, manic defence and paranoid delusions—[that] allows one unconsciously and consciously to think about and make psychological use of experience. A person unable [to dream] to learn from (make use of) experience is imprisoned in the hell of an endless, unchanging world of what is."

This view of the function of dreams presents an inversion of the relationship between conscious and unconscious experience described in the archeological model of dreams. The archeological model assumes that dreaming is a universal aspect of psychic functioning and that "dream work" consists of undoing processes of repression and disguise while for the transformational model "dream work" is thought of as a developing capacity to contain, enrich, and affectively elaborate experience developing subjective, unconscious meanings. Ogden (2004a, p. 1356) believes that "Freud's dream work allows derivatives of the unconscious to become conscious, while Bion's work of dreaming allows conscious lived experience to become unconscious (i.e. available to the unconscious for the psychological work of generating dream-thoughts and for the dreaming of those thoughts)" and that the goal of psychoanalysis is facilitating the development of the capacity to dream. He states:

> A person consults a psychoanalyst because he is in emotional pain, which unbeknownst to him, he is either unable to dream (i.e. unable to do unconscious psychological work) or is so disturbed by what he is dreaming that his dreaming is disrupted. To the extent that he is unable to dream his emotional experience, the individual is unable to change, or to grow, or to become anything other then who he has been. The patient and analyst engage in an experiment within the terms of the psychoanalytic situation that is designed to generate conditions in which the analysand (with the analyst's participation) may become better able to dream his undreamt and interrupted dreams . . . In the course of participating in dreaming the patient's undreamt and interrupted dreams, the analyst gets to know the patient in a way and at a depth that may allow him to say something to the patient that is true to the conscious and unconscious emotional experience that is occurring in the analytic relationship. What the analyst says must be utilizable by the patient for purposes of conscious and unconscious psychological work, that is for dreaming his own experience, therefore dreaming himself more fully into existence. (p. 857)

In this very pointed definition of psychoanalytic psychotherapy, Ogden develops Bion's concept of dreaming as the activity of the unconscious mind similar to Schore's (2011) concept of the right brain as the center for processing affective experience and the left brain as the center for processing external events. Bion's theory of thinking evolved from his early papers which focused on thinking and the disruption of the ability to think, to his highly abstract idea of alpha function, which was a mode through which raw sensory and affective experience, concrete paranoid schizoid experiences, are transformed into meaningful, personal thought processes. Bion next developed the concept of the container contained, which was an explicit intersubjective theory of thinking that emphasized the mother or therapist position as being able to tolerate and transform the child or patient's unacceptable, evacuated experiences into meaningful symbolic experiences. Bion's container contained model of thought is both intersubjective and intrasubjective. He thought of the inability to contain painful thoughts[3] as involving evacuation, projective identification without someone willing to introject or contain the unwanted thought.

Lastly, and in keeping with contemporary models which think of the mind as involving parallel rather than hierarchical structures, Bion thought of the unconscious as an apparatus of dreaming in which emotional experiences are continuously being processed in parallel with conscious understanding of experience. Bion referred to this function as waking dream thoughts, a developmental achievement of the capacity to dream which Ogden is utilizing in the previous quote as the patient being able to dream "himself more fully into existence." In a similar and perhaps less poetic use of Bion's theories of waking dream thoughts, Grotstein (1979) describes the development of a "dream screen" and defines one of the therapist's tasks as repairing the rips and holes in the dream screen to help his/her patient be able to dream their experiences and create personal meaning.

Birkstead-Breen (2009) discusses the intersubjective aspect of mother's and infant's or patient's and therapist's creation of meaning as a joint process of dreaming or reverie. She describes this as "reverberation time" which leads to a subjective sense of time and suggests that failures in this process lead to deficiencies in the area of representation and mentalization. She suggests that such deficiencies lead to a tendency to act out, rather than to be able to think and tolerate the passage of time. Ferro (2006, 2008) has written a great deal about Bion's concept of dreaming which he suggests redefines the psychoanalytic enterprise from a psychoanalysis of contents and memories to a psychoanalysis that gives priority to the development of the apparatuses for dreaming, feeling, and thinking. Like many other theorists, Ferro (2009) raises the question of working with patients who have not developed the capacity for reverie or alpha function, and are unable to engage in the creation of personal meaning through the waking dream process. He states:

> In the absence of this capacity to transform proto-emotions and proto-sensoriality into pictograms (of the waking dream state), the analyst will need to cooperate, perhaps even using his own reveries, in the coconstruction of the patient's α-sequences, thus enabling the patient to develop an α-function and containing capacity (♀) of his own and eventually allowing its stable introjection. (p. 218)

CLINICAL ILLUSTRATION

The following clinical illustration describes the development of the capacity to use waking dream thoughts, reverie, and alpha function in a patient who was unable to enter into dream states and therefore unable to create personal affective meaning. He is consistently oriented toward an asymmetrical, functional view of the world and is focused on action.

This patient was unable to dream, or use processes of reverie to affectively elaborate his experiences which were described simply as hard facts, "reality." William was a successful orthopedic surgeon who had several failed attempts at psychoanalytic psychotherapy. He came to this current therapy after a recent breakup of a long term relationship with a woman for whom he had little passion or respect. As William described this relationship and previous relationships with woman he focused on sequences of difficulties, external events with few references to his own or his partner's feelings, intentions, and motivations. He reluctantly reported that he had bouts of contentless panic and depression for which he had taken medication in the past.

William was clear that he did not believe in therapy and wanted to see results quickly. He was concerned that becoming introspective, in his words "staring at his navel," would interfere with his ability to make decisions and to act decisively. It seemed as if he lived almost exclusively in the external world of facts and actions. The only affect and sense of aliveness that I felt in the first sessions occurred when he described his passion for heli-skiing. As he talked about those experiences, I could feel his excitement and pleasure in his competence, in nature, and in being alone with the ever-present possibility of injury and death.

William grew up in the Rocky Mountains and had a clipped and direct way of speaking. He was athletic, pragmatic, thoughtful, principled, and decisive. He was quite critical of most of his colleagues, particularly his superiors, which led to frequent difficulties in his professional relationships. He had issues with authority and seemed to be both counterdependent and counterphobic. He described his family as somewhat rigid and religious, having many rules, and discouraging discussions of feelings, fears, difficulties and anxieties. He remembered a repetitive childhood dream, more like a night terror, in which a big soft blob progressively fills the room, suffocating him, and he wakes up in a wordless state of terror. He had no memory of being comforted by his parents either when he would be awakened by this dream or at other times in his childhood.

Ogden (2004b) describes several disturbances in the ability to dream, including night terrors, like William's, which are undreamt dreams; literal dreams, which neither patient nor analyst can associate to; and nightmares which are interrupted dreams. Night terrors (Ogden, 2004b, p. 860), like William's, are "raw sense impressions related to emotional experiences (beta elements) which cannot be linked in the process of dreaming, thinking or storage as memory" and reflect pockets of psychotic experiences or experiences that are foreclosed from affective and symbolic elaboration in dreams or in reverie.

It is helpful to think about concepts such as alpha function, dreaming, linking, and reverie, as transformational processes which organize and create meaning utilizing systems of logic, rules of combination and relationship, which function like computer programs that create meaning out of sets of data, raw experience. Matte-Blanco (Matte-Blanco, 1988; Newirth, 2003) describes two parallel transformational systems based on different forms of logic. The first, asymmetrical logic, organizes and generates experience in the external world, through differentiating the four dimensions of reality: person, place, time and causality. The second, symmetrical logic, organizes and generates unconscious experiences such as dreams, reverie, poetry, art, and intimate relationships through effacing differences, and using condensation, displacement, similarities, metaphors, and evocative presentational symbols. I thought of William as having a well developed capacity to use the asymmetrical logic of external reality and the world of work, but not having developed the capacity to use the symmetrical logic of dreams, unconscious experiences, and intimate relationships.

Ogden (2007) describes his work with several patients who, like William, have not developed the symmetrical capacity to dream, and are stuck in the asymmetrical world of material reality, facts, and action. He describes his analytic approach, "talking as dreaming," in which content that would seem to be disconnected from personal experience, having minimal analytic relevance, becomes affectively elaborated by the analyst and subsequently by both the patient and analyst. In expanding the kinds of content that become incorporated in the analytic discourse, Ogden emphasizes the development of the patient's capacity to dream, focusing on the analyst's symmetrical processes of reverie in creating a dream space in which the patient's concrete asymmetrical experiences can be contained and affectively elaborated. Ogden (2007, p. 577) describes talking as dreaming, as "an experience of the patient's coming into being in the process of dreaming his lived emotional experience; and the analyst and patient thinking about and at times talking about, the experience of understanding (getting to know) something of the meanings of the emotional situation being faced in the process of dreaming." Talking as dreaming becomes a way of infusing asymmetrical experiences with symmetrical, metaphorical, dream-like images, facilitating the patient's development of the capacity to dream.

William and I set out on our analytic adventure, he committed to a pragmatic, asymmetrical approach to life and I committed to a symmetrical strategy facilitating his capacity to dream, to elaborate and link his inner experience with his external life, using symmetrical, symbolic, evocative metaphors. We began focusing on the difficulties in his relationships with women, with closeness and with trust. William had a hard time with the symmetrical nuances and subtexts involved in romantic and professional relationships. As our relationship evolved I found myself talking like, enacting the role of a coach, using various game metaphors as a way to move from the "he said—she said" of his reports of the facts of a conversation to a dream-like world of power, strategy, intention, fears and feelings. Often he felt that my game metaphors did a disservice to his more principled and idealistic view of the right and wrong of relationships. Through our talking as dreaming about interpersonal relationships as games, William became more able to enter the symmetrical world of intimacy and dreams, developing a deeper appreciation for himself and others. Rather than presenting a transcript of our psychoanalytic dialogue, I would like to present three moments in our relationship which illustrate William's evolving capacity to "dream himself into existence."

During the time when I was "being a coach" and he "a competitor," I felt that he would often reject my interventions and interpretations with a "so what" or "show me" attitude. He reported the following dream, challenging me to tell him what it meant. He dreamt that he had cut off his penis and put it in the outside hanky pocket of his suit jacket as he was going into a meeting with administrators of his hospital. As he told me the dream, his attitude, his nonverbal communication, enacted the narrative of the dream. He threw down the gauntlet demanding that I tell him what this dream meant. He was simultaneously counterdependent, counterphobic, vulnerable, frightened, and curious. In this analytic moment I had many thoughts; I thought of the content of the dream as a caricature, a psychoanalytic trope, castration anxiety, and authority; I also thought that this dream asked the question of whether it was safe for him to enter the world of dreams without losing or giving up an important part of himself, and lastly I thought that it represented his aggressive, self-destructive and combative approach to the world. I also knew that I could not, not respond to his demand, and that I had to tell him what it meant rather than stereotypically asking him what he thought that it meant. I said that I thought that the dream reflected his need to proudly disempower himself, castrate himself, because of his fear that someone else would do it—I continued, saying that you do it to yourself before someone else can and then cockily say look at me. This interpretation led to his becoming more relaxed in the session and more connected and aware of the counterphobic aspect of the way he organized his life. From the perspective of the dream as a transformational process, this literal dream left little room for associations and elaboration outside of being an intense, graphic representation of the way that he had acted in much of his life and his anxieties about being in our therapeutic relationship. However, his request, demand, that I interpret his dream also reflected an implicit, procedural, now moment. It was like a request for me to acknowledge his need, could he trust me or would I make fun of him, could I contain his terrible and disowned anxieties about authority, powerlessness, and castration.

The next moment that I want to describe occurred as we moved toward a more collaborative analytic relationship. William started the session saying that he had a dream the previous night and that although he was not sure what it meant it had felt good to him. In this dream he was a ski instructor and he was teaching, perhaps coaching, his old mentor, with whom he had had both a great deal of difficulty and also held in high esteem. The feeling that he reported in the dream and the way it was told was quite different from the previous dream. It was collaborative and we both seemed to be free to associate to the many possible meanings of the dream. My comments had to do with his feeling that he wanted to be able to be giving and be recognized by an authority. I wondered whether he saw a parallel in his relationship with his mentor and with me. This dream seemed to mark a change in our relationship and William's ability to enter into the symmetrical world of dreams and metaphors where we could each use reverie to affectively elaborate our experiences. The content of this dream, particularly in relation to the previous dream, could be thought of as a movement from a counterphobic "I'll do it to myself, before you can" competitiveness, castration anxiety, and difficulties with authority, to a collaborative albeit wary approach to the power differentials of authority relationships, and a more complex set of identifications as both a son and a father. Switching from the dream content to the dream process, this dream represents a shift in William's capacity to dream, to link experiences, use reverie and metaphor in more hopeful, collaborative ways, linking multiple internal and external relationships.

The last analytic moment that I want to describe was not a dream; it was William's talking like dreaming, introducing a metaphoric experience into our relationship. We had been working together for about 2 ½ years and although we both seemed to feel that the work was going quite well, William consistently began sessions stating his reservations about therapy and his feeling that we should be thinking about ending in the near future. One day he began a session by saying with a smile that he has come to see therapy as the opposite of fast food. When I asked what he meant by that, he said: "I always look forward to having fast food and then after I eat, I feel disappointed and empty. While I always hate coming for therapy, but after a session I always feel that I have gotten a great deal, a lot to think about and feel deeply satisfied." After a moment, I responded more spontaneously than intentionally, saying that's how I feel about going to the gym; I always hate going and can never remember how good I feel after a workout.

I think of my spontaneous comment as a symmetrical interpretation in which I recognize our similarities, and the difficulty and struggles involved in both psychic and physical growth. We both laughed and went on with the session. We continued talking in metaphors, each using our experience to elaborate ways that we have come to stretch and enrich ourselves, using dream-like images to transform external experience into meaningful internal experience, looking forward in an intentional, committed, and hopeful way. It did not seem important or necessary to move from this symmetrical dream-like conversation into a discursive, asymmetrical conversation that would attempt to explain our interaction which had been clearly articulated in our choice of metaphors. It is interesting that our choice of metaphors and metaphoric interactions involved the physical activity which was important to William. These choices represented both symmetrical and presentational processes as contrasted with a more asymmetrical discursive interpretive strategy. William was developing the capacity to dream both in his waking life and in his dream life; he was becoming able to use the transformational processes of dreaming in organizing, linking, generating, and creating his world, and to be able to dream himself into existence.

CONCLUSION

These three clinical moments illustrate the development of dreaming as a transformational process; focusing on William's growing capacity to dream his undreamt and interrupted dreams, to use the symmetrical, metaphorical processes of reverie, and to link his experiences in an affectively meaningful way. Rather than focusing on the content of his dreams, issues of authority, castration anxiety, competitiveness, and power, this paper focuses on the development of William's capacity to dream, to use unconscious transformational process in linking and enriching conscious experience with unconscious symmetrical symbols in the development of subjective meaning and intimate relationships. These processes are difficult to articulate, because they bring both analyst and patient into a changing, uncertain, symmetrical dreamscape of illusions, metaphors, and the nuances of intimate relationships. I hope that this case illustrates the importance of the capacity to dream, and to dream oneself into existence as a necessary condition for the development of self-knowledge and truly knowing another.

NOTES

1. Martin Luther King, Jr., I Have a Dream, delivered 28 August 1963, at the Lincoln Memorial, Washington D.C.
2. Freud's interpretation of the Wolf Man's dream is a dramatic example of this view of dreams.
3. Bion, like many object relations theorists, uses the concept of thought to stand for affective experiences which need to be understood, reflected on, and symbolized. He implicitly separated the capacity to think about the external world and the internal world as described in the previous chapter. His concept of thinking/thought is always referring to the affective internal world of experience.

Chapter Four

Humor as a Universal Human Emotion

Humor and jokes have often been thought of as useful tactics in establishing the psychoanalytic and psychotherapeutic relationship, or as a means of communicating painful insights within an affectively warmer context. Jokes and humor, like other art forms, have always been part of human experience and culture, which suggests that humor represents something more essential, more universal, then a therapeutic tactic. Humor like Winnicott's (1971a) idea of play, or Fonagy's and Target's (1996) concept of the pretend mode of thought, seems necessary for the development of the capacity for symbolic thought, mentalization, empathy, emotional connection, and mutual understanding. Before turning to the clinical use and the intersubjective experience of jokes and humor in the psychotherapeutic relationship, I want to look at these processes from several theoretical perspectives to further understand the intersubjective and intrasubjective structural aspects of the importance of jokes and humor in creating the mind and its capacity for symbolic thought. I extend Freud's (1905) concept of "joke-work" in terms of Matte-Blanco's, Klein's, and Lacan's theories and discuss the use of jokes and humor in psychoanalytic treatment as a means of interpreting, organizing, perceiving, and generating unconscious meaning and profound intersubjective experiences of connection and understanding.

FREUD'S EVOLVING VIEW OF HUMOR AND JOKES

Freud (1905) described jokes, humor, and wit as unconscious productions, universal experiences, like dreams, in which processes of condensation and displacement organize and generate deep emotional meaning. He suggested the concept of joke-work, as parallel to dream-work, in order to explain the unconscious process through which perceptions, drives, and affects are "pulled into the unconscious" and result in the creation of jokes, moments of disinhibition, of pleasure, of controlled as well as uncontrolled laughter. Freud's concept of joke-work, like his concept of dream-work, involved a structural approach through which he explains the complex affective and cognitive processes involved in the unconscious creation of meaning.

Freud (1905) catalogued jokes by form, by technique, and by purpose, and compared them to dreams, constantly deepening his argument that both dreams and jokes provide an understanding of the unconscious mind and the importance of the nonrational, nonlinear thought processes of condensation, displacement, and indirect representation. Freud underlined the spontaneous, involuntary, and unbidden nature of jokes, which reflect their origin, like dreams, in the unconscious mind:

> We speak, it is true, of "making" a joke; but we are aware that when we do so our behavior is different from what it is when we make a judgment or make an objection. A joke has quite outstandingly the characteristic of being a notion that has occurred to us "involuntarily." What happens is not that we know a moment beforehand what joke we are going to make, and that all it then needs is to be clothed in words. We have an indefinable feeling, rather, which I can best compare to an absence, a sudden release of intellectual tension, and then all at once the joke is there—as a rule ready-clothed in words. (p. 167)

Freud highlights the spontaneous experience of "making a joke" as something which emerges fully formed in words, often not quite rational, often representing an ironic or sarcastic perception of a current situation. In this way jokes, like dreams, seem to develop in and emerge from a part of the mind which we may associate with the unconscious or seemingly as a right brain function.

Freud (1905, p. 179) described the social or interpersonal nature of jokes as different from dreams, which he thought of as an "antisocial mental product . . . a compromise between the mental forces struggling within" a person which necessitated an effort to remain unintelligible and disguised. He also highlighted an intersubjective dimension, the importance of the other, in the creation of jokes. It is unusual for Freud to highlight the importance of the listener, which is a forerunner to contemporary intersubjective views of mental processes. Freud observed that laughter is among the most highly infectious expressions of psychic states:

> When I make the other person laugh by telling him my joke I am making use of him to arouse my own laughter; and one can in fact observe that a person who has begun by telling a joke with a serious face afterwards joins in the other person's laughter with a moderate laugh. Accordingly, telling my joke to another person would seem to serve several purposes: first, to give me objective certainty that my joke work has been successful; secondly, to complete my own pleasure by a reaction from the other person upon myself; and thirdly—

> where it is a question of repeating a joke that one has not produced oneself—to make up for the loss of pleasure owing to the joke's lack of novelty. (p. 156)

Freud's understanding of the intersubjective, affective, and symbolic aspect of jokes and humor was limited by his view of the mind as a contained, energy discharge system in which affect arousal implied a potentially dangerous situation that required either inhibition or a moderate pleasurable discharge to maintain the individual's psychic balance and relation to reality. This one person conflict model of the mind did not allow him to fully develop the importance of jokes as a two person intersubjective, emotional, and cognitive organization of experience. However, in a brief later paper, Freud (1927, p. 166) returned to his interests in jokes as he seemed to move away from this one person model of the mind centered on the inhibition and discharge of drives. In this paper he suggests a new understanding of jokes and humor, developing an early version of object relations theory, in which the superego functions like a kind parent reassuring a frightened child: "Look! Here is the world, which seems so dangerous! It is nothing but a game for children—just worth making a jest about!"

Freud (1927) began this later paper, "Humour," with a joke in which he describes an individual's triumph over adversity. Interestingly, Freud (1905) presented the same joke in his earlier work, which seems to suggest its importance and a special pleasure in telling this joke which he does not comment on. Freud's (1927, p. 161) repetitive joke: "A criminal who was being led out to the gallows on Monday remarked: Well this week is beginning nicely." I believe that Freud's repeating this joke reflected his identification with the criminal as both an outsider and as one who challenges authorities, and ultimately has the last laugh.[1] This paper suggests an incipient shift in Freud's view of the individual's relation to reality, of the function of the superego as an internal object, and a different set of goals for psychoanalysis. Freud (1927) now seemed to conceptualize humor as a potential asset, a synthetic process, a means for the individual to triumph over the inevitable limitations of life, suffering, and external reality. This view suggests a constructive view of narcissism which values idealization, merger, and presents a positive view of omnipotence. Like the following Buddhist koan, this joke about the criminal reflects an important paradox, both the shortness of life and the eternity of a moment.

In a Buddhist koan, a young monk is being chased by a hungry tiger; he reaches a cliff and is about to jump to safety when he sees below him several hungry tigers. Hanging over the cliff, barely within reach, is a fragile branch with one perfect strawberry dangling off the end. What is he to do? How is he to escape this dilemma, his fate? The monk jumps and grab the fragile branch and enjoy the perfect strawberry as he falls through space to his encounter with the hungry tigers, with his fate, with the Lacanian real. This koan, like Freud's joke, emphasizes the necessity to take pleasure in one's circumstances to transcend the universal experiences of limitation, persecution, powerlessness, meaninglessness, and insignificance.

HUMOR AND THE LACANIAN REAL

From a Lacanian perspective (Dor, 1998, p. 69), jokes are unconscious formations that combine metaphor and metonymy, condensation, and displacement. Lacan (1996) viewed humor as an important aspect of the individual's developing capacity to address the limitations imposed by society, mortality, and the unspeakable terrors of the real. Lacan (1996, p. 313) compared the relationship between action and desire within the psychosocial structures of tragedy and comedy. For Lacan, the essence of tragedy is the triumph of death, the willingness of the tragic hero to choose death as an expression of choice and dignity in a confrontation with the Real. In contrast, Lacan viewed comedy as an unconscious structure that expresses the individual's capacity to choose life in an encounter with the real, with the limits of existence. Lacan stated:

> One must simply remember that the element in comedy that satisfies us, the element that makes us laugh, that makes us appreciate it in its full human dimension, not excluding the unconscious, is not so much the triumph of life as its flight, the fact that life slips away, runs off, escapes all those barriers that oppose it, including precisely that are the most essential, that are constituted by the agency of the signifier (language) . . . . Life goes by, life triumphs whatever happens. If the comic hero trips up and lands in the soup, the little fellow nevertheless survives. (p. 314)

Zizek (1991) describes sociopolitical events from a Lacanian perspective and argued that comedy is an extremely powerful way to symbolize those aspects of human experience (the Real) that leave us speechless and horrified. He illustrated this aspect of comedy with a discussion of two films about the Holocaust, an unexplainable and unspeakable horror, which he believed can best be understood through comedies such as Robert Benigni's 1997 film *Life is Beautiful*, and Lina Wertmüller's 1975 film *Seven Beauties*. These films confront the question of how we might understand and symbolize the Holocaust without sacrificing the subjective experience of its emotional reality for a more objective and coherent historical narrative involving explanations and abstractions. Zizak suggested that in comedy, when the subject, such as the hero in *Seven Beauties*, continues to maintain the absurdity of his survivalist stance, through attempting to seduce the sadistic and purposely unappealing commandant, eventually our laughter stops and we come to experience the desperation, powerlessness, nausea, and disgust that is at the center of this experience of the Real, unmediated by abstract thought and explanation. Similarly, the father in *Life is Beautiful*, convinces his son that the concentration camp that they are in is simply a game, a form of play and not the horrific place that the audience is well aware of. For Zizek, like Lacan, and I believe Matte-Blanco, comedy paradoxically provides us with the ability to faithfully symbolize the emotional, unconscious experience of the Real, of the horrifying and terrifying experiences that make us feel helpless, meaningless, empty, and dumb.

BI-LOGICAL ASPECTS OF JOKES AND HUMOR

Matte-Blanco's (1975, 1988) development of the bi-logical theory of conscious and unconscious experience is useful in extending Freud's theory of jokes and humor. Matte-Blanco hypothesized two separate modes of apprehending and knowing the world. Conscious organizations of experience are based on the use of asymmetrical or Aristotelian logic through which we perceive, organize, and generate our understanding of differences and distinctions among persons, places, time, and causality. Unconscious organizations of experience are based on symmetrical logic in which differences among persons, places, time, and causality are effaced and similarities are perceived, organized, and created. Asymmetrical logic is the logic of science, the law and objective rational experience, whereas symmetrical logic is the logic of dreams, poetry, art, humor, and subjective emotional experience. The difference between conscious or asymmetrical thought and unconscious or symmetrical thought can be understood functionally, with asymmetrical thought used to understand, denote, differentiate, and elaborate objective aspects of reality and symmetrical thought used to perceive, evoke, and create similarities and elaborate subjective aspects of reality. Matte-Blanco's concepts of symmetrical and asymmetrical thought are quite similar to Langer's (1942) description of discursive and presentational symbols and the neuro and cognitive psychology's descriptions of implicit and explicit organizations of memory and thought.

One characteristic of symmetrical logic is that it treats an object, thought, or experience as if it were part of an infinite mathematical set in which each member of the class is identical to all others and represents an unlimited, identical number of experiences. This infinite quality of thought is particular relevant for emotional experience which led Matte-Blanco to conceptualize emotional experience as symmetrical, unconscious experience in which a person in a dream may stand for many people who evoke the same emotional experience. The infinite quality of unconscious experience is related to the emotional qualities of timelessness, absoluteness, and the never-ending aspects of subjective experiences. Matte-Blanco (1975) illustrated the relationship between the infinite quality of symmetrical emotional experience through examining the subjective experience of love:

> When someone loves, his feeling transcends the particular moment and wraps his whole person in a peculiar non-temporal (infinite) state of mind. A young man in love would not express his feelings adequately if he were to say to his beloved: "I love you for this limited moment of time and then I shall love you no more." An outsider or even he himself (as a spectator of himself) may know that this emotion is a passing one, but when he feels it, he feels it as something that will last forever. (p.245)

Matte-Blanco's discussion of love illustrates the critical difference between the asymmetrical structure of external experience and the symmetrical structure of internal emotional experience. As in the Buddhist koan, and Freud's joke, humor and jokes can be understood as symmetrized structures which reflect the infinite nature of subjective emotional experiences in which one moment represents all moments of time and existence.

Matte-Blanco (1988, p. 72) presents the argument that asymmetry and symmetry are parallel modes of processing information and experience and that "the same reality is simultaneously treated . . . as if it were divisible or heterogeneous formed of parts, (within the asymmetrical mode) and on the other, as if it were one and indivisible (within the symmetrical mode)." Although Matte-Blanco did not describe his bi-logical system as either a system in which experience is simultaneously processed in parallel structures, this model would seem to fit quite well with current neuropsychological, cognitive, and developmental perspectives on processing information and the creation of meaning. In clinical practice we are often struggling with and attempting to understand and transform a patient's deadened, asymmetrical experience of self and other into an alive, vital, symmetrical affective experience of self in relation to the other, through processes of interpretation and the development of the capacity for reverie and dreaming. Bi-logical theory recognizes that this process of interpretation is not simply a process of making the unconscious conscious but of bringing the infinite depth of unconscious experience and affects into experiences that are organized in the asymmetrical mode.

INTERPRETATION, JOKES, AND THE UNCONSCIOUS

Rayner (1995) described interpretation from a bi-logical perspective as a form of mapping unconscious experience into language and suggested that these maps are most useful when "imbued with bi-logical structures, such as emotionally loaded language, metaphor, other figures of speech, jokes and poetry" (p. 166). Rayner discussed the use of jokes, which are symmetrized bi-logical structures, as talking to "the patient using the language of the unconscious" and stated (Rayner, 1995, p. 124) that "interpretations in the forms of jokes, etc., can be the closest and most appropriate mapping of the unconscious at a particular moment." Rayner illustrated the use of humor with a joke that Matte-Blanco told a patient who had cancelled the previous appointment because of "having the flu and being afraid to infect the analyst." Through telling his patient a joke, as opposed to an explanation or traditional interpretation of resistance, Matte-Blanco expressed the unconscious meaning of the patient's actions and consciously experienced anxiety, by introducing a symmetrical dimension within a strongly asymmetrical analytic relationship. He created a shared moment of pleasure and a profound emotional experience of the current transference situation.

Matte-Blanco told the patient that his concern about infecting the analyst reminded him of a joke in which "a man suffering from delirium tremens was being interviewed by a psychiatrist. This patient complained of the itches 'of bugs' and kept brushing them away toward the psychiatrist who said 'For god's sake, don't brush those things on me'" (as cited in Rayner, 1995, p. 124). The patient laughed, probably seeing aspects of his own behavior reflected in this joke, a symmetrized, bi-logical structure. Subsequently, Matte-Blanco suggested a more asymmetrical interpretation, which was that his patient also wanted to frighten him into thinking that he would be infected so that he would tell the patient not to come to the following session.

This joke, like other symmetrical experiences that have an infinite quality, suggests many meanings and emotions that could have been contained in this therapeutic moment. We may think of this joke as reflecting a universal fear of infecting or poisoning the other with our toxic substances and wishes, a Kleinian image of the envious baby at the breast. In telling this joke in the context of this particular transference relationship, Matte-Blanco reversed the role of aggressor and victim, caricaturing his own position and creating a more fluid and accepting attitude toward the patient's unacceptable, destructive affects and wishes. This can be seen as an example of containing and transforming the patient's unacceptable fears of destructiveness and allowing the patient to reinternalize their previously unacceptable feelings. Typically interpretation is thought of as altering the patient's internal life; however, in telling a joke the analyst also transforms the intersubjective structure of the transference-countertransference relationship. We may see this intersubjective aspect of jokes as facilitating a move from the paranoid schizoid organization of the transference, to a depressive organization of the transference, in which both patient and analyst move beyond the paranoid position of victim and persecutor into a depressive position in which there is an integration of love and hate and an experience of mutual identification transcending the personal boundaries of history and time. Schlesinger (1979), writing about humor and identity, suggests that with humor the "distinction between victim and audience is minimized and their identification (with each other) is more or less complete" (p. 318).

TWO-DIMENSIONAL MODEL OF MENTAL EXPERIENCE

In chapter 2, I presented the Matrix of Psychic Experience (Newirth, 2003), a two-dimensional model of mental experience that integrates the bi-logical dimension of symmetry—asymmetry with the Kleinian dimension of the paranoid schizoid and depressive positions. The Matrix of Psychic Experience illustrates an important aspect of the process of projective identification in which an internal experience becomes experienced as an external event. When a person uses projective identification to externalize unacceptable feelings and thoughts these feelings and thoughts become experienced as part of the external world and are organized and perceived within the framework of asymmetrical logic, as external, concrete, persecutory objects. To address the clinical, interpretive, and transformational aspects of asymmetrical and symmetrical organizations of experience I suggest two broad interpretive strategies—an asymmetrical strategy and a symmetrical strategy. In the asymmetrical strategy we use discursive language to explain and differentiate aspects of the patient's historical and external experience, facilitating the patient's development of the capacity for abstract thought, inferential thinking, and objective self-observation. In the symmetrical interpretive strategy we use evocative, presentational language to facilitate patients' ability to move beyond the paranoid position of victim and persecutor and develop the capacity for symmetrical symbolic experiences, such as dreams, metaphors, poetry, humor, and self-reflective thought.

The use of jokes and humor in psychoanalysis creates a symmetrical interpretive strategy which has two functions. It facilitates the patient's capacity to transform externalized paranoid and unconscious concrete emotional experience into metaphors that generate new experiences and perspectives, and simultaneously transforms the relational structure of the analytic dyad creating a fluid transference-countertransference relationship. For example, Matte-Blanco's use of humor in elaborating and mapping the unconscious emotional meaning of his patient's concerns and fears of infecting him transformed the relationship from an asymmetrical mode in which the patient and analyst were well-defined, separate individuals, each with their own role in the social hierarchy, functioning in an investigative, scientific mode, to a symmetrical relationship in which there is a loss of boundaries between who is superior and who is subordinate, between present situation and the one described in the joke; each becomes both persecutor and victim, in an infinite set of therapists and patients, of toxic wishes and fears of infecting and being infected.

The use of jokes and humor in analytic treatment develops the symmetrical bi-logical structures that transform unconscious concrete affective experiences, functioning like dreams, metaphors, and poems, simultaneously symmetrizing the relational structures, bringing together two people in a new more egalitarian relationship in which there is a loss of temporal and spatial boundaries, and an intense pleasure in the transformation of and triumph over the paranoid schizoid experiences of helplessness, powerlessness, isolation, and the limits of external reality. In the following section I present examples of the clinical use of jokes, humor, and the comic to illustrate the transformation of unconscious experience and the symmetrization of intersubjective relationships.[2]

CLINICAL ILLUSTRATIONS

Many authors (Schimel, 1978; Poland, 1990; Baker, 1993; Strean, 1994) emphasize the value of humor in reaching difficult patients, particularly those in which the transference-countertransference relationship is skewed toward paranoid schizoid organization involving splitting, sadomasochism, idealization, and the depreciation of the analyst. Bader (1994, p. 28) noted that many of these patients seem to be highly resistant to traditional (asymmetrical) explanations and interpretations and "require a more visceral and affectively undeniable demonstration from the analyst that the relationship was safe enough to risk real analytic exploration." Bader (1994) described his work with a difficult and demanding patient who expressed a great deal of dissatisfaction with the analysis while demanding that the analyst provide him with concrete help with his current life events. This patient had sought analysis for help with his relationships with women, which "became sadomasochistic, with increasing covert and overt battles for control and a growing sense of despair." Bader came to understand his own difficulty with the frustration and despair in the evolving transference-countertransference relationship as a derivative of his relationship with his own mother "who had often burdened him as a child with her complaints of being cheated and dissatisfied as a mother and wife" (p. 31).

As a result of his process of reverie and his understanding of this concrete symmetrization between the patient and his mother, Bader was able to modulate his helpless feelings and his withholding affective style and introduce a more playful and humorous style in which he sometimes was self-mocking and sometimes confirmed his patient's accusations in a caricatured, humorous and playful way. For example, the patient would make a sarcastic comment like, "Did they teach you in school to make interpretations that your patients can't understand or use?!" to which he would respond, "Do you think I went to school to learn how to do this?" or "Yes—it was in the same course where they taught me to blame the patient for my mistakes" (p. 31). Bader's use of self-deprecating humor reflects several transformations into a symmetrized experience from a closed, concrete, paranoid, despairing transference-countertransference relationship that emphasized an asymmetrical interpretive strategy to a more hopeful relationship in which both analyst and patient use humor to express their paradoxical experiences of hate and love, dependence and independence, rejection and desire, and hope and disappointment in an evolving symmetrized relationship.

Bader's countertransference experience of the patient's criticalness and disappointment as concretely the same as his mother's is an example of both the infinite experience of emotion, and of paranoid or pathological symmetrization. Bader's ability to shift to the use of humor in a symmetrical interpretive strategy reflected a form of depressive symmetrization in which there is movement from a concrete paranoid mode to a more playful one in which unconscious meanings can be generated through the enactment of the fantasy of the disappointed child and the sadistic, inadequate mother. In this second symmetrization it is not only the unconscious that becomes symbolized by the use of humor but also the relationship that has become symmetrized so that the role of the analyst and the role of the patient become exchanged in an alternating symmetrized experience of dominance and submission. Bader's example suggests that an analyst's use of humor is not a simple intentional, voluntary act but as in a dream or other unconscious experience it reflects a creative resolution of a disjunction between conscious and unconscious organizations of living reflected in the transference-countertransference relationship, where there is an experience of intense frustration in the defined asymmetrical roles of analyst and patient.

Pasquali (1986) presented an example in which this transference–countertransference disjunction is expressed in the despair of being unable to resolve the patient's sadistic attacks, which led to a seemingly spontaneous, humorous approach in which she was able to shift from an asymmetrical interpretive strategy to a symmetrical interpretive strategy. Pasquali described the analytic experience in the following way:

> "A" starts off the session attacking me in a subtly cruel way, then goes on to torture me to a sadistic crescendo; the more I try to hold my head together and find a channel of communication to stop the passion which makes "A" totally dominated by his hatred of me, the more sadistic "A" becomes. All my efforts are killed from the start, the atmosphere becomes very heavy, the hope of finding a way out minima. I am struck by an image "A" evokes just in the middle of his sadistic attacks: a lizard, the tail of which "A" skillfully chops off. I see myself dressed up in green, like a lizard; furthermore I perceive myself desperately trying to create a new thought to replace the one "A" has just chopped off. Smilingly I say to "A": "It is a very well known fact that, like the lizard's tail, the analyst's head grows, after every new attack, newer and

> stronger then ever." "A" laughs; the atmosphere changes radically. We have both been able to perceive our own absurdity: "A" who takes pleasure in seeing my head grow again soon after he has cut it off with sharp words: I clutching at my arm chair, telling myself that I must stand up at any cost, that I must find a new explanation: the new one must certainly be the right one. (p. 233)

This transformational moment in the analytic dialogue illustrates Winnicott's (1971a) concept of the importance of surviving the patient's attacks and the shift from object relating to object usage. But like other examples of the use of transitional experiences in analysis, humor is a function of the symmetrization of the analytic relationship, a merging or dedifferentiation of the unconscious experiences of both analyst and patient that results in a pleasurable moment of mutual identification, a diminution of the asymmetry of the roles of analyst and patient, and a symbol of the unconscious meanings of the transference-countertransference fantasy into the analytic dialogue. Jokes and humor symmetrize the analytic relationship, creating deeper emotional meanings that are based on subjective experiences and personal insights.

I want to describe a moment in which the emergence of a humorous comment, a joke, provided a new insight into the transference-countertransference relationship and shifted the analytic relationship from the repetitive complaints of the patient as an injured victim to joining the analyst as the persecuting other. The patient spent many sessions over the preceding months, complaining about her stepdaughter's extraordinary entitlement. In attempting to address her obsessive, negative response to this adolescent behavior we focused on the contrast between her feelings of resentment and deprivation as a child and her stepdaughter's feelings of entitlement and demands for constant indulgence. However, this insight did nothing to reduce my patient's complaints and experience of personal outrage. The sessions became litanies of the latest entitled demands and acts, which I experienced as extremely repetitive, boring, and emotionally distancing. I began feeling as helpless and powerless as my patient felt in her current and childhood homes. The patient's self-righteousness pressed many personal buttons for me. In the midst of a series of repetitive, emotionally deadening complaints I had the image of the patient and myself as prosecutors/persecutors at the House Un-American Activities Committee and jokingly made reference to the McCarthy hearings by saying "I have an envelope in my pocket with the names of the Communist sympathizers." The patient immediately understood my humorous reference, laughed, and shifted her perspective from that of a resentful victim of her stepdaughter's demands to enjoying the power of her previously disowned persecutory, self-righteous, judgmental self. In this moment of laughter and pleasure we became one symmetrized critical and judgmental voice that facilitated a shift in understanding, symbolizing our unconscious experiences of envy and destructive criticism while feeling the absurdity of the superior, pseudo-parental potions that we had each assumed in our attempts to be the grown-up mature one in contrast to the whiny, entitled child that our transference-countertransference situation had propelled us into enacting.

DISCUSSION

These examples of the use of jokes and humor in psychoanalysis and psychotherapy illustrate several dimensions of the symmetrization of emotional experience. Initially, in each example, there was a dedifferentiation of the transference and countertransference so that both patient and analyst found themselves encapsulated in an asymmetrical, concrete world of persecutory anxieties. These deeply frustrating, despairing, and persecutory experiences become resolved through the analyst's capacity for reverie, containment, affective elaboration and entering the symmetrical symbolic mode of organizing experience where a joke or humorous comment emerges and reframes the formerly disowned feelings of both patient and therapist into an experience of pleasure, connection, and triumph over the limits of the real. These examples present an important dimension of technique, the therapist's choice to utilize a symmetrical interpretive strategy instead of the more typical asymmetrical strategy of interpretation in which experiences of person, place, time, and causality are differentiated and used in developing temporal explanations. A symmetrical interpretive strategy effaces differences in the dimensions of the external world creating an infinite space of emotional experiences within the psychoanalytic and psychotherapeutic relationship.

The use of humor, like dreams or other symmetrical processes, facilitates the patient's development of the capacity to symbolize unconscious experience and mitigates the need to evacuate unconscious experiences and fantasies into the external world in processes of pathological projective identification. Humor takes many forms in relation to different clinical situations, including mutually created jokes, caricatured enactments, cartoon-like images, and self-depreciating commentary on the analytic process. In using jokes and humor in psychoanalysis we introduce the possibility of pleasure within an intense, intimate moment which allows for the transformation of unacceptable aspects of both patient and analyst as they become joined within a broader human experience.

Either member of the therapeutic dyad may introduce humor into the dialogue. Patients who are able to enter into the depressive position, who have developed more articulated internal and external relationships, will often introduce humor and jokes through poking fun at either themselves or the therapist. Patients who are in more paranoid schizoid states and are extremely concrete, present experience in states of psychic equivalence, experience their life in terms of victim and persecutor, and see therapy as extremely hierarchical, are often unable to use humor, and because of an experience which Bion (1959) described as attacks on linking, the therapist is also unable to use humor or other symmetrical strategies in the treatment situation. In these situations it is often the therapist who eventually becomes able through processes of reverie to introduces humor which symmetrizes the transference-countertransference relationship, merging or dedifferentiating the unconscious experiences of analyst and patient. In the clinical examples the use of humor often articulated the very concrete, destructive transference-countertransference relationships in which the therapists experienced a disruption in their capacity to think, to form links and metaphors, reflected in their countertransference experiences of boredom, rage, fear, and terror. These analysts struggled with their countertransference and were often able to use humor, choosing a symmetrical interpretive strategy, through which they developed interventions that caricatured themselves in their experience of the transference-countertransference relationship. These therapeutic symmetrical moments reflect early stages of the transformation of concrete paranoid schizoid experience into symbolic, depressive position experiences introducing the possibility of mutual recognition and the beginning capacity for reflective function. In each clinical moment the therapist was able to identify with and affectively elaborate the disowned evacuated parts of the patient through a process of symmetrization. Matte-Blanco became a comical, fearful, and cranky psychiatrist. Bader became an outrageous, rebellious, and uneducated analyst. Pasquali became a cartoon character regenerating her head over and over again. I became a caricature of a paranoid, grandiose prosecutor who knew everybody's secrets. In these examples, the analyst introduced symmetrical experiences through self-mocking caricatures, cartoon-like images, enactments that transform the previously concrete deadened and destructive transference-countertransference relationship.

Symmetrical interpretive strategies involve a movement into a fluid, unconscious, and often paranoid world in which there is a loss of boundaries as we attempt to symbolize the now-merged transference-countertransference relationship. As we move away from asymmetrical, discursive strategies in which we explain events to patients and use symmetrical, presentational strategies in which verbal and nonverbal enactments are used to create affective experiences, identifications, enhance the dyad's and patient's capacity to play, and develop the capacity for symbolization and mentalization. The comforting distinctions of the asymmetrical world becomes left behind: concepts of person, place, time, and causality become a whirling blur, as we lose our sense of subject and object in the humorous enactment and the momentary pleasure and excitement of the now moment. However, not every joke leads to a successful symmetrization of the transference-countertransference relationship. Many fail, and some hurt the patient. It is hoped that these hurtful, disruptive experiences present opportunities for reparation and greater mutual understanding and connection. Like other failed now moments (BPCSG, 2007) these failed attempts to use humor can be part of the therapeutic cycle of rupture and repair leading to a greater capacity for symbolization. The choice to use humor, like play or other symmetrical strategies such as transitional experiences, involves the willingness to live with paradox and to take the risk of exposing one's subjectivity and unconscious fantasies. Jokes are both true and not true; we cannot ask an individual to explain his or her joke without radically altering its meaning. For example, was Matte-Blanco actually afraid of being infected by his patient or was he dramatizing his fantasy of himself and his patient, or expressing his secret identity? However complex its origin, Matte-Blanco's joke was a volitional enactment through which he symmetrically gave voice to his experience of the transference-countertransference experience.

We can never know why a particular joke emerges with a particular patient at any one time. With each joke the analyst chooses a symmetrical strategy, introducing a dimension of pleasure while revealing aspects of his or her inner world. I clearly enjoyed the opportunity to become a paranoid, grandiose prosecutor/persecutor who knew everybody's secrets, when I "spontaneously" made a reference to the McCarthy hearings. A joke introduces a potential experience of intense affect and pleasure into the analytic relationship, which might test the parochial and "scientific" limits that we have imposed on our professional behavior. However, the capacity to use jokes and humor in approaching the limitations, tragedies, and finality of life has been a part of psychoanalytic and human wisdom throughout the ages. I believe that the experience of analytic transformation can only be achieved through the experience of acknowledging the pleasure and acceptance of those unacceptable and disowned parts of ourselves that we find at the core of jokes and humor. The use of humor and jokes in the therapy relationship illustrates a fundamental emotional process through which people overcome their alienation and separateness, become coupled when two or more individuals become joined in a single affective moment which is felt to extend infinitely through a double process of intrapsychic and intersubjective symmetrization. This double process of symmetrization underlies all emotional, intimate, intersubjective relationships. Humor and laughter is one medium that allows for the loss of the burden of individual identity (see Searles, 1979, for a further discussion of this last point) and creates moments of transcendence over the limits of biological, psychological, and physical reality, allowing for the creation of loving relationships and the development of deep personal meanings and commitments.

NOTES

1. After Freud was released by the Nazis he added a postscript to the letter he was forced to write exonerating his captors and stating that he was treated well by the SS. He said something like: "I recommend the SS for their hospitality to whomever would avail themselves of it."

2. The symmetrization of intersubjective relationships may be a way of thinking about the development of Ogden's (1994) and Benjamin's (2000) concepts of the analytic third.

Chapter Five

Pleasure in the Transitional Space

Intersubjectivity and Transformation

INTRODUCTION

In the previous chapter we discussed jokes and humor as part of a larger theory of transformation and of the dual, parallel structure of the mind. In discussing jokes and humor, pleasure became a central aspect of the transformational process. This chapter will approach pleasure as a critical aspect of the process of transformation and the development of the capacity for symbolization and mentalization.

Often there are unexpected moments when we become joined with our patients in pleasurable, joyful, or ecstatic experiences. These *now moments* (Stern et al., 1998), whether spontaneous or intended, are powerful fulcrums in the change process. Often, they are the critical things remembered, forming the history of an analysis while stimulating the courage to leave the safety of the past and move into an unknown future. I think of these moments of pleasure as symmetrizations (Matte-Blanco, 1988) of the analytic relationship: dream-like processes, reverie, playful transitional experiences, metaphors, and poetic experiences involving condensation and the dedifferentiation of time, person, place, and causality. Symmetrizations occur when we enact transference-countertransference fantasies, depart from our usual analytic mode by telling a joke, singing a song, or experience and possibly express an affectionate, loving, or erotic feeling. However, these symmetrical moments of mutual pleasure, joy, or ecstasy can be frightening; we experience a loss of professional distance, our analytic position becomes insecure, we become concerned with what our colleagues might say, our parental superegos enter the consulting room and fill us with self-doubt. Pleasurable symmetrizations are often experienced as moments of loss of professional identity, during which transference and countertransference become confused and we may no longer know, "is this me?" or "is this him/her?" Until recently (Davies, 1998), psychoanalytic theories have avoided discussing such frightening countertransference feelings and enactments, and instead have equated pleasure with infantile pursuits or inappropriate sexual experiences with the belief that the analytic relationship should provide as little gratification as possible for both patient and analyst.

Celenza (2010) addresses the issue of pleasure in the psychoanalytic relationship, discussing the guilty pleasures and anxieties of erotic countertransference as well as the importance of multiple levels of engagement, which I describe in the clinical illustration as a symmetrical or metaphorical enactment. She (Celenza, 2010, p. 181) believes that "our patients do not really want us to gratify their erotic wishes despite their vociferous protests to the contrary. But they do not want us to simply maintain our professional role either. This was the mistake of the abstinent classical analyst who refused to allow his patients to know him personally. What our patients want is not an engagement from within one single dimension (i.e., the role, the person, the professional, or the woman) but to have the multiple roles coalesce into one." Davies (2003) wisely put it, "in healthy families, the oedipal conflict is both won and lost. Just how is this done? I would venture to say that the parent conveys, 'I would if I could,' or, 'in another time or place.' This is what we need to convey to our patients." Similarly, Frieda Fromm-Reichman (2015) in responding to a disturbed patient who pressed her to date him outside of their professional relationship responded in a manner that was both empathic and limit setting, both symmetrical and asymmetrical. Fromm-Reichman said that "perhaps had they met under different circumstances they might have dated, but because they met as therapist and patient it would not be possible."

In this chapter, I explore the powerful transformative potential of moments of pleasure, as well as the fearful countertransferential anxieties generated by symmetrical experiences in the psychoanalytic relationship. I argue that the analyst's ability to create moments of pleasure with a patient facilitates the patient's development of the capacities for concern, love, and self-acceptance, as well as the ability to symbolize and integrate aspects of the self that may have felt unwanted or disowned by the patient and his/her parents.

BEYOND THE PLEASURE PRINCIPLE

In Freud's early writing, pleasure was viewed as one side of the central conflict human beings face and need to protect themselves from by subordinating the pleasure principle to the reality principle. With the development of the structural model, Freud placed the superego in the position of the reality principle in order to regulate the ego and id. Freud (1930) consistently viewed sexuality and pleasure as a riptide that pulls us away from civilization and toward the world of the primal horde, of incest, and murder. In this conceptualization, the pursuit of pleasure would lead to the loss of our capacity for rational choice and the destruction of civilization.

Though Freud did not critique his earlier views on the dangers of pleasure, in "Beyond the Pleasure Principle" (Freud, 1920) he addressed the idea that people are often not motivated by either the pursuit of pleasure or by mature rational thought, but instead repeat painful experiences in which they seem to pursue unhappiness and misery. Freud (1920) began his essay, "Beyond the Pleasure Principle," by discussing the limitations placed on the pleasure principle, reiterating the idea that the presence of external danger necessitated its subordination to the reality principle. The second limitation that challenged Freud's understanding of the importance of the pleasure principle was the traumatic and war neuroses. The symptoms of these neuroses did not fit the theory of the pleasure principle; for example, patients who experienced trauma were frequently awakened in states of terror by dreams which repeated their traumatic experiences. Freud (1920) did not believe that these dreams could be interpreted as wish fulfillments and argued that, "the function of dreaming, like so much else is upset in this condition and diverted from its purposes" (p. 13).

Freud developed the concept of the repetition compulsion to conceptualize the painful symptoms of the traumatic and war neuroses. He normalized the repetition compulsion, presenting a charming discussion of his grandson's *fort da* game, which he believed was the method through which his grandchild mastered the painful emotions which resulted from his mother's absence. Freud understood this game as a model in which an overwhelming distressing event, experienced passively, is mastered through repetition, turning it into an active pleasurable experience. After discussing the *fort da* game, Freud (1920, p. 21) turned to the repetitive nature of transference, describing how "patients repeat all of these unwanted situations and painful emotions in the transference . . . [in which they] contrive once more to feel themselves scorned, to oblige the physician to speak severely to them and treat them coldly." He concluded: "none of these things can have produced pleasure in the past, and it might be supposed that they would cause less unpleasure today if they emerged as memories or dreams instead of taking the form of fresh experiences." Freud presents these transference experiences, as well as the repetitive unhappy experiences which individuals not in analysis attribute to fate or bad luck, as evidence for the existence of a repetition compulsion.

Freud did not maintain the purely psychological direction suggested by his grandson's *fort da* game, namely the importance of pleasure in mastering the repetitive painful experiences of the traumatic and transference neuroses. He seemed to need an additional biological explanation, and he developed the theory of the death instinct to explain the pervasive self-destructiveness that he observed. In developing the theory of the death instinct, Freud reiterated psychoanalysis's phobic attitude toward pleasure. This fearful attitude toward pleasure remains active in many contemporary theories. For example, Mitchell (1997), in addressing the theme of why we are compelled to repeat unhappy experiences, suggests that experiences of pleasure are inherently disruptive and frightening, necessitating avoidance and directing the individual toward the safety and security of his/her known world. He suggests that the repetition of unhappy relationships represents safety, while pleasure is experienced as a fearful and threatening possibility. A patient poignantly illustrates this phobic attitude toward pleasure; he described his choices which have maintained a life of unhappiness and despair, as his fear of letting go of the safety of a sinking, rotting, smelly raft in order to swim the relatively short distance to a beach filled with good food, beautiful women, sunshine, and a joyful life. Green (1995) strongly criticizes contemporary psychoanalysis's phobic attitude toward pleasure arguing that pleasure and sexuality which are at the heart of psychoanalytic thinking has been lost or severely marginalized. This fearful attitude toward pleasure and the safety of repeating the unpleasure of the past may be seen in the traditional metaphor: "the devil you know is better than the devil that you don't know."

Phenomenological Approaches to Pleasure:

Kohut (1984) is among the few American analysts who introduced the concept of pleasure as a positive, constructive element in human development and in analytic relationships. He emphasizes the importance of parents' expression of "joyful" or "prideful" recognition of the developing child's budding sexuality and assertiveness. He (Kohut 1984) comments on the parallel importance of analysts' attitudes of joy, happiness, and pride in their analysands' progress and achievements and reminds us that we should warmly acknowledge these feelings without fearing that our joyful attitude represents illicit gratification of the patient's malevolent or infantile desires.

Kohut (1984) challenges the restrictive attitudes of his classical colleagues in his description of his work with a forty-year-old university professor with whom he agreed to postpone "the payment of (his) fees for several months because the professor wanted to make a down payment on some property in a Colorado resort" (p. 73). He believes that this enactment affirmed the professor's hope that this new analysis could be for him and not for the analyst. Kohut focuses on the importance of agreeing to the patient's request, an archaic self-object transference, an enactment, which was subsequently understood as representing important historical and transference dynamics. Although the treatment was successful, it leaves us with an uncomfortable feeling because there is too much pleasure in this enactment: the pleasure of a vacation home in the Colorado mountains, the pleasure of not paying one's analyst, the pleasure of indulging a patient, and the pleasure of transgressing the rules of analysis.

Davies (2003, 1998), in a more direct challenge to our institutional prohibitions of pleasure and sexuality in the analytic relationship, discusses her participation in erotic transference-countertransference enactments with two patients. In these transference-countertransference situations she thoughtfully recognizes and works through her erotic feelings and the prohibitions against these feelings which represent frightening enactments and repetitions of her patients' family experiences, as well as a transgression of her own psychoanalytic principles. Davies argues for the recognition of the importance of normative aspects of sexual fantasies in analysts, patients, parents, and children. She conceptually and experientially differentiates these symbolic experiences from actions in external reality.

Davies (1998) furthers her argument by describing "benign" and "malignant" forms of seductiveness in terms of the analyst's capacity to recognize and be responsible for his/her own participation in the erotic transference-countertransference enactment. What is most interesting and admirable about Davies's approach is her use of the analytic situation as a "place" in which adult, not infantile, sexual desire can be freely played with without it being reduced to a therapeutic ploy or an overly sentimental experience; rather moments of intense pleasure and fear are openly experienced by both analyst and patient. After carefully facilitating the exploration of her patient's anxiety-filled experience during which he felt she was flirting with him, Davies (1998) differentiates the repetitive transference aspects of this enactment from the progressive movement into new regions of adult sexuality:

> You thought I was flirting with you . . . that's not about you being a little boy . . . wanting the me you can't have. That's about seeing me responding to you as a man . . . recognizing that I am a woman. What's so scary about this place is not that you can't have me . . . that's old hat . . . we've talked about that so many times before. The scariest thing about this place . . . about playing and flirting in this place . . . is that here in this moment, in this particular place and in this particular way, we can have each other as man and woman . . . we have the potential to enjoy it and to each watch the other enjoy it. And that's a much scarier, much more grown up thing for us to manage responsibly. (p. 762)

In focusing on erotic feelings, Davies simultaneously challenges and maintains the psychoanalytic tradition of equating pleasure within the psychoanalytic relationship with the dangers of sexuality. She challenges us to expand our awareness, recognize and be responsible for our experiences of sexual desire as we facilitate our patients' (and our own) development into more creative capacities for adult love and sexuality. However, her focus on oedipal issues supports the traditional model in which sexuality is primary and pleasure is a secondary or derivative experience. In my view, pleasure is not a derivative of the sexual aspects of these experiences, rather it is inherent in the creation of a "place," a playground in which sexual and nonsexual play can occur as mutual affective and effecting experiences, where patient and analyst join together in creating a transitional, symmetrical, symbolic experience.

The "place" that Davies develops, much like Freud's grandson's *fort da* game, involves transforming a passive, persecutory experience into an active, joyful, symmetrical game in which there is a reversal of roles and the generation of multilayered intersubjective meanings. Davies's multileveled use of the phrase "a man and a woman" echoes a marriage vow, while her description of each watching the other's expanding experience of pleasure generates a "now" moment. This "nowness" effectually refocuses the dialogue from the asymmetrical, discursive (Langer, 1942) verbal mode which presents historical explanations, to the symmetrical, presentational mode of implicit relational knowing, which evokes for both the patient and reader the mutual, sensual, visual, and kinesthetic experience of intimate relationships and adult sexuality. The pleasure in this enactment is not simply that of a sublimated or denied sexual experience, but that of a symmetrical, metaphoric, poetic moment, a moment of deep understanding and transformation in which new intersubjective meanings are generated and the immediacy of this experience is timeless; a remembrance of things past which are always being created in the present. In order for such transformations to occur, pleasure must infuse the analytic experience as the nucleus of an exciting and frightening now moment in which the transference-countertransference relationship becomes enacted and expressed in a symbolic symmetrical mode. Davies's patient is able to simultaneously be desired and desiring; this complex, intersubjective form of pleasure becomes created, and no longer needs to be dissociated or disowned in the transference relationship and in the patient's life.

Bromberg (2008) expands Kohut's (1984) and Davies's (1998, 2003) spontaneous enactments describing them as critical analytic processes for working through patients' dissociative, concrete, nonreflective states in which they repeat their flight from the pain of unregulated affect storms, tsunami-like experiences, which underlie the necessity for dissociation. Bromberg describes how dissociative experiences impair patients' capacity for reflective, symbolic thought processes leaving them in states of avoidance, deadness, which protects them from experiences of affective storms stimulated within current relationships. He (Bromberg, 2008) describes unplanned moments, collisions in the analytic relationship as "safe surprises" through which patient and analyst are able to "distinguish the likelihood of mental shock that could be indeed affectively overwhelming from the kind of excitingly edgy experiences that are always interwoven with the risk of spontaneity" (p. 329). Bromberg's concept of safety involves both spontaneous playful, nonlinear engagement and a highly egalitarian (symmetrical) relationship in which his patients feel free to comment on, be critical of, the collisions and negotiations which occur between them. For example (Bromberg, 2008), one patient with whom he wished to have a more lively exchange than their usual flat, concrete conversation suddenly responded to him in a surprising and ironic way, shifting the level of discourse from the concrete to the symbolic; "with a twinkle in one eye and a glare in the other said, 'I think you are starting to have delusions of *candor*.' I broke up in laughter and so did she" (p. 336). This now moment helped overcome the dissociation which existed in the patient and in the analytic relationship, allowing for the development of a greater capacity for symmetrical, symbolic experience, for transitional experiences, real play and pleasure in the analytic relationship. I want to underline the experience of pleasure and joy that occurred in this moment when patient and analyst are joined together in laughter as a critical element in the process of transformation which Bromberg describes.

SUBJECTIVE SYMBOLIC DIMENSIONS OF PLEASURE

Lacan (1998) differentiates experiences of simple pleasure from more complex symbolic, subjective, and intersubjective experiences of pleasure which he describes as jouissance. Simple pleasure involves a reduction of physical or psychological discomfort, a return to a homeostatic state, while jouissance represents complex symbolic experiences, which like mentalization involves an intersubjective experience, being the object of the other's desire while simultaneously desiring the other. The desire to be desired by an other creates the potential for both intensely pleasurable and intensely vulnerable experiences in which an individual is dependent on an other's mental or symbolic experience for pleasure. Lacan focuses on the intersubjective, symbolic aspects of jouissance (complex pleasure) and desire, as well as the frightening and vulnerable aspects of these experiences. He (Lacan, 1998) describes the inevitable dilemmas and dangers of intersubjectivity and pleasure, our need for recognition, our desire to be desired, to exist within another's mind (consciousness), as the Master Slave dialectic, in which the master is dependent on the slave's freedom to choose and recognize the master. Bob Dylan (1979) poetically captures the inevitable vulnerability and anxiety inherent in the Master-Slave dialectic in his song "Gotta Serve Somebody."

Lacan (1998) describes the ecstasy, ambivalence, anxiety, and terror that accompany intersubjective states of pleasure, as they propel an individual toward wanting to be desired by another, while simultaneously being threatening with fragmentation and the loss of self as he/she becomes subject to the other's desire, to the possibility of becoming enslaved and or made to feel dead.[1] A way to imagine the fear and pleasure which accompanies desire and jouissance is to think of moments in which desire brings us to an intensely pleasurable experience in which we fear losing our self, as when we are tickled to the point where pleasure feels on the edge of pain, or in orgasm, where pleasure becomes too intense and needs to be stopped immediately.

Intersubjective pleasure is a complex symbolic experience in which pleasurable experiences are linked with, or perhaps more accurately, are linked within, the subjective experience of the other; we desperately want to be and are terrified of being held within the other's symmetrical, symbolic world. Davies's (1998) patient's multidimensional question illustrates the complex intersubjective, symbolic, exciting, and frightening experience of pleasure and desire: "'Forgive me if I'm wrong,' he said, 'but I think you're flirting with me'" (p. 761). This question reflects the patient's wanting and not wanting affirmation for his experience of his therapist's sexual desire, experienced nonlinguistically as an implicit, procedural, relational experience. Intersubjective moments of jouissance, like this, involve desire, anxiety, and dread; it is as if we ask in the (now) moment that we enter the intersubjective world of pleasure: will I be experienced as bad and destructive, will I be loved and accepted, will I experience ecstasy or will I be lost in a whirlpool of pleasurable and destructive emotions?

SYMMETRICAL SYMBOLIC EXPERIENCES

Contemporary two person, relational, Kleinian theorists[2] conceptualize the mind as a transformational system, extending Bion's (1962) concept of reverie, the container contained model, and Winnicott's (1971a) concept of transitional experience. Both Bion and Winnicott developed Klein's (Klein, 1946; Segal, 1978) concept of symbolization within the paranoid-schizoid and depressive positions (see chapter 2). These authors understand the function of unconscious processes, such as reverie, transitional experience, and dreams as transforming, passive, persecutory, concrete experiences of the paranoid schizoid position into active, subjective, symbolic experiences of the depressive position. We may think of these transformational processes as complex elaborations of Freud's observation of his grandson's *fort da* game. Following Bion, Ogden (2010) and Grotstein (2000) describe these processes as waking dreams in which parallel conscious and unconscious processes are continuously attempting to transform concrete experience (beta elements) into symbolic experiences (alpha experience). Pathology is understood as the inability to use reverie, dreams, and symmetrical symbolic processes to elaborate and link emotional experience with useable symbols and metaphors to create personal meaning.

Matte-Blanco (1988), following Bion, developed Freud's concepts of primary and secondary process thought by focusing on different ways that information and meaning are apprehended, experienced, and generated. He suggested that secondary process thought primarily operates on information from the external objective world using asymmetrical or Aristotelian logic, which differentiates experience in terms of time, person, place, and causality. Primary process thought operates on internal, unconscious, and affective experiences and is generated and organized using symmetrical logic. Let me illustrate these two forms of logic using hypothetical interpretations of the same transference experience in which a patient treats the analyst as his/her mother. An asymmetrical interpretation would attempt to differentiate the past from the present and the analyst as a current object from the historical object through stating, "I am not your mother." Alternatively, a symmetrical interpretation would collapse differences in time, person, and place by entering more deeply into an affective, dream-like, metaphorical experience; in this case the analyst would state, "I am your mother." Both statements are true, though each develops a different experience in the analytic relationship. The asymmetrical interpretation attempts to reestablish a more reality-oriented experience, differentiating the present relationship from a past real or wished-for relationship. The symmetrical intervention ("I am your mother") can be thought of as the analyst inviting the patient to join him in a transitional experience of play, much like Fonagy's and Target's (2007) shared pretend mode, a "now moment" which alters the explicit relational configuration through an evocative, implicit, procedural experience. It is hard to imagine making a symmetrical interpretation like "I am your mother" without speaking in an ironic or puckish tone, adding a dimension of pleasure and affective complexity to the symmetrical interpretive process. The child development literature (Mancia, 2006) refers to these nonverbal aspects of communication as qualities of markedness, which define the important non-literal aspects of implicit communication that contribute to the child's capacity for mentalization while understanding implicit relational structures and intentionality.

Fonagy (2008) presents an interesting and relevant theory of the development of sexual pleasure which like Lacan's idea of jouisance emphasizes the intersubjective dimensions of pleasure and the critical importance of being contained in an other's body and mind. Although Fonagy's discussion primarily focuses on the development of the capacity for sexual pleasure it can also apply to the broad spectrum of intersubjective pleasure. Fonagy (2008) begins with the observation that experiences of sexual arousal and pleasure are difficult for the parent to mirror and therefore remain uncontained, an unspoken and unspeakable alien force or object in an unarticulated or dissociated unconscious. Although describing early attachment relationships the following statement (Fonagy, 2008, p. 25) can also describe the importance of reflecting pleasurable experiences with patients in analysis: "Each partner is, momentarily, both alone and fused with the other. Secure, playful, mutually mentalizing interaction with the caregiver (therapist), nurturing the imagination, is a key precondition of the kind of intersubjectivity that psychosexuality entails. Attuned secure parenting (therapeutic engagement) generates the interpersonal context for an erotically imaginative intercourse, while its content arises out of the adaptive mother-infant missattunement. (I)t follows from our hypotheses that reciprocity is key."

CLINICAL ILLUSTRATION

I want to illustrate the dangers and creative potential of shared moments of pleasure in my work with an unhappy, schizoid woman who found herself in repetitive situations in which she felt deprived and persecuted by what she thought of as her fate, the impersonal forces of life, and society. The psychoanalytic transformational approach I describe combines contemporary two-person relational psychoanalysis with Kleinian and Lacanian structural models that focus on developing patients' capacity for symbolic, symmetrical, subjective thought[3] which underlie the ability to enter into intimate intersubjective relationships in analysis and life. This focus on the development of intrapsychic structures (capacities) extends the phenomenological self-psychological and relational approach in two ways: first, intervention focuses on the development of the capacity for symbolic thought, self-reflection, mentalization, and compassion, in addition to new object experiences which contrast with repetitive prior relationships. Second in this approach, the analyst attempts to optimize symmetrical as compared to asymmetrical interventions, developing a playful, metaphorical, dream-like, experience in the analytic relationship. In this example, I focus on the development of symmetrical, symbolic experiences of pleasure and desire, which like Lacan's concept of jouissance exist on the edge of a whirlpool of sensual images, symbolic discourse, and the loss of clear definitions of analyst and patient, self and other. This illustration can be thought of as moving between safety and surprise (Bromberg, 2008) as the patient and I develop several extended metaphors which both deepen the analytic relationship and facilitate the development of the capacity for symbolic thought.

Samantha experienced herself as a deprived "have not" in an impersonal schizoid world in which fate was always against her. Samantha came to therapy feeling deadened, in a schizoid-like state in which she complained of having little pleasure in her life, an inability to desire or expect success or happiness. She described her life as filled with repetitive experiences of self-sacrifice, loneliness, deprivation, incompetence, and inadequacy. She could not understand why she was unable to develop a long-term committed relationship with a man. Samantha is an attractive Asian woman in her mid-forties who is divorced with no children, and works as an attorney in a government agency. She grew up in the Midwest where she was the second of three daughters. Although Samantha understood that her experiences of unhappiness reflected long-standing conflicts, including her ambivalence about being a woman, her identification with her self-sacrificing mother, and her belief that her desire was destructive, these insights were only marginally useful ideas that made sense but had little effect on her day-to-day experiences, capacity for joy, relationships with men, or her experience of desire. For her, the belief that desire was dangerous and that she is an overwhelmed, anxious, unhappy, lonely, deprived woman was an unalterable reality.

Samantha remembers being close to her father, a stern, angry, and critical man; however, this close relationship ended when she reached puberty. She described her mother as extremely "thin," both literally and metaphorically; she frequently shopped in thrift stores, and was self-sacrificing, confused, and never expressed desire. Finding her mother's life as a suburban housewife abhorrent, Samantha did not initially see herself as identified with her mother; however, she has been both surprised and saddened to recognize many aspects of her mother in her own difficulties with pleasure, desire, ownership, and achieving happiness. Samantha's experience of desire tends to be absent; she presents herself as overwhelmed, struggling to keep her head above water, unable to have relationships with men, and blames herself for her lack of happiness and success.

Samantha's difficulty achieving success and happiness seems to be related to the intertwining of gender and desire which was represented in a repetitive adolescent fantasy in which her sexual desires are externalized while she experiences herself as passive, paralyzed, unable to move or act. In her adolescent fantasy, she is taken to a mining camp during the gold rush in California, tied to a post, wearing a revealing dress while a crowd of miners leer at her, making lewd, sexual comments that make her feel both excited and threatened as if she will be raped. Samantha remembers having this fantasy frequently and found it to be both exciting and scary. Samantha's fantasy, which seems to reflect her disowning of her sexuality and an affirmation of her fear of desire, is strikingly similar to a fantasy presented in the movie *Belle du Jour* (Baum, Hakim, & Buñuel, 1967). In this scene, the protagonist, a woman, who is unable to experience desire, sexual arousal, or pleasure, imagines herself tied to a tree and beaten[4] by a workman.

Samantha has not developed the capacity for reverie, and as she continues to live in a functional, asymmetrical world of events and facts, she is unable to transform her concrete affective experiences (beta elements) into symbolic experiences (apha function); she instead evacuates and disowns all potentially pleasurable experiences. This evacuation of her inner experiences reflects a lack of the capacity to use symmetrical symbolic processes, self-reflection, or mentalization. She is trapped in an asymmetrical, concrete world in which her language remains largely descriptive and discursive, organized in the mode of the psychic and symbolic equivalence, and is without affect, elaboration, personal meaning.

In our sessions, Samantha describes her sense of inadequacy, being overwhelmed and frightened at work, and never having time to enjoy herself. She often contrasts her own life and experiences with an idealized view of my perfect and pleasure-filled life. Although Samantha wishes to have a relationship with a man, she has felt unable to make efforts to engage in social activities, angrily insisting that "there are no men out there" or that the only available men are "losers." As we have analyzed her sense of impoverishment and her inability to develop a relationship with a man, we have come to understand that she had a strong unconscious belief (Britton, 1995) that her desires were toxic, that if she liked a man and fantasized about a relationship, her fantasies and desires would make him die or disappear.

Finding a way to resolve the split between Samantha's conscious experience of deprivation and her paralyzing, unconscious belief that her desire is destructive and toxic was the critical issue in our work, and is one that highlights questions about the efficacy of insight in psychoanalytic treatment. I think of this split as one between experience as organized with asymmetrical logic, which provides explanations and differentiates the present from the past, and experience organized with symmetrical logic, as in dreams, poetry, and art, which create metaphors and symbols that allow us to experience multiple aspects of our selves and escape from the concrete repetitions of the past. Rather than viewing the analytic situation and the transference-countertransference relationship as exclusively an opportunity for developing discursive, narrative understanding through asymmetrical interpretations and differentiating the past from the present, I think of it as an opportunity to symmetrically enact and metaphorize the patient's disowned unconscious concrete beliefs. The analytic space becomes a stage upon which the patient and I can develop transitional experiences through playing out and symbolizing those fearful experiences which keep people like Samantha imprisoned in concrete, restricted, alienated, hopeless, and fragmented worlds. It is important to recognize that these symmetrical experiences are often associated with pleasure; they are ironic experiences which allow both patient and analyst to "laugh at themselves" in the theater of unconscious resonance, repetitively enacted in both analysis and in life.

It is very hard to predict or explain why a particular event emerges at a point in an analysis and not earlier or later. In analysis, now moments (Stern et al., 1998) occur organically, possibly reorganize the transference-countertransference relationship, transform ongoing, repetitive, deadened facts into alive now moments after which the analytic relationship takes a new direction. Two events occurred in close proximity which intensified Samantha's unconscious envy and disowned desire. After I returned from a mid-year vacation, Samantha told me of a colleague who she felt superior to, and their conversations about how this individual was juggling several men and was having a great time socially. It was hard for Samantha to express her envy, and she denied both her negative feelings about my vacation and her colleague's "exploitive" relationships. Samantha kept returning to her well-worn themes of not having money like me, and disparaging her colleague's dishonesty with men. Although we had analyzed similar situations in the past, this time I was struck by Samantha's pride in her ability to survive with so much debt and so little pleasure.

Without conscious intent I became preoccupied by a fantasy which I initially tried to put aside, but when this thought persisted I began to symmetrically elaborate it. I began to mentally play with the opera *Porgy and Bess* (Gershwin, Gershwin, and Heyward, 1935), thinking of the scenes, themes, and music, alternatively distracted by the feelings of guilt and pleasure which came from this reverie. As this process of reverie continued, I began to listen to Samantha from a new symmetrical perspective, and imagined our analytic relationship recontextualized by my reverie of *Porgy and Bess*; I thought of myself as "Sportin' life," the greedy drug dealer, who always seemed to be having fun, was free to act on his desires and take whatever he wanted. As I elaborated my reverie, I heard the lyrics "I got plenty of nothing and nothing's plenty for me" (Gershwin, 1934a) I continued to struggle, still feeling distracted by my fantasy, until finally I thought, "well, this is Samantha's song"; I then began to imagine our relationship as an enactment of *Porgy and Bess*. In work with patients I often introduce my fantasies and reveries, seeing them as a way of expanding the content of sessions to include unconscious derivatives and initiating a process of transitional relatedness. These associations often include cultural references such as songs, plays, movies, and current events which the patient may or may not be familiar with but that tend to expand the context of the analytic discourse. Ogden (2007) writes about the use of cultural experience in the development of analytic meaning between himself and patients.

Although I had no conscious reason to think that Samantha would know this opera, I asked her if she knew *Porgy and Bess*, and she did! I gleefully suggested that her song was "I Got Plenty o' Nuttin," which goes, "I got plenty of nothing and nothing's plenty for me . . . ." (Gershwin, 1934a). I asked her to sing it and to both of our astonishment, she did. As she sang, I was surprised at how natural it felt for her to be singing this song. As she sang/enacted "I got plenty of nothing and nothing's plenty for me" her experience of pride and pleasure in her choice to have nothing became clear, that having nothing was paradoxically a success rather than a failure. I realized that I also had a song to sing, that in our enactment of the unconscious transference-countertransference fantasy about pleasure and desire as good and evil, I had my own identifications and secret pleasures, and that my song was "Summertime . . . and the living is easy" (Gershwin, 1934b) I told her that this was my song and sang as much of it as I knew, expressing the joy in having whatever I wanted and basking in the warmth and fullness of summer. This pleasurable and playful session ended and we both felt moved, excited, and deeply satisfied.

In the following sessions, which took on an extremely pleasurable feel, we sang and discussed these two songs; hers reflected her lack of joy, disowned desire, and pride in self-sacrifice and self-deprivation, while mine reflected the joys of summer, greed, desire, and transgressing the law. We discussed her accurate perception of my pleasure in vacationing and other ways in which I felt free to flaunt my enjoyments. These songs and the unconscious fantasies of desire they represented became transitional experiences, ways in which we joyfully enacted Samantha's lack of desire, her self-sacrifice, and her disowned pride. Often when Samantha would return to her recitations of having nothing, I would suggest that she "sing her song" or alternatively I would sing a few lines from "Summertime." Our relationship became infused with the songs and characters of *Porgy and Bess*. These songs became a special language between us, a set of transitional experiences through which Samantha represented, symbolized, and transformed herself in relation to experiences of pleasure, desire, and being a woman. Like Freud's grandson, these songs became transitional experiences, intersubjective opportunities to transform her concrete repetitive experiences of deprivation into symbolic, active, symmetrical experiences of personal meaning and pleasure.

These mutually created, symmetrical, and transitional experiences which we playfully enacted in the pretend mode transformed our relationship as well as important aspects of Samantha's life. As the analytic relationship evolved and Samantha became more accepting of pleasure, desire, and experiencing herself as a woman, I suggested that she might have a new song: "I Enjoy Being a Girl," to which she immediately responded that she thought that her song might be "I Feel Pretty" (Rodgers & Hammerstein, 1958; Sondheim, 1957). In sessions over the next months, Samantha suggested other songs as both representing and transforming her experience of pleasure, desire, and femininity. At one point she suggested that her song was "You Can't Get a Man with a Gun" and in what seems to be the last song in this sequence "House on a Hill" (Berlin, 1958). These symmetrical symbolic enactments became the language of our psychoanalytic relationship and facilitated Samantha's capacity to feel desire, more entitled to pleasure, and more comfortable being a woman. During this period she met and developed a relationship with a warm, interesting man who she eventually married.

However, the pleasure and movement in these sessions eventually stalled and the repetition of her sense of deprivation and unhappiness returned; one opera was not going to completely transform Samantha's phobic relationship with pleasure and her commitment to unhappiness. Samantha returned to her sense of herself as deprived, as being a "have not" in spite of growing evidence to the contrary. Our sessions lost the sense of aliveness that the transitional experiences surrounding *Porgy and Bess* had provided. It felt more like we were trudging through a heavy, gray, inhospitable landscape which we dutifully pushed through with little hope. In one session, as Samantha was expressing the repetitive themes of deprivation and poverty, the title and first line of the song "Miss Otis Regrets" intruded into my awareness (Porter, 1934). I asked Samantha if she knew that song; she had a vague sense but did not really know it. I also did not know the song and felt that my association reflected my experience of Samantha politely declining to be emotionally present in our sessions and in her life. However, when I looked up the lyrics of this song, I was quite surprised to find that it described a relationship in which Miss Otis kills her lover who has betrayed her. I felt frightened by these lyrics, as if it was an unconscious premonition, a prediction that she will murder/leave her lover or me. I also thought that it may reflect my jealousy of her new relationship and my own murderous feelings. It is interesting that this song which I had enjoyed during the previous session and which brought Samantha and I together momentarily had now turned shameful and frightening. Neither of us brought the song up in the next or the subsequent sessions. We both seemed to not want to enter into that fantasy and returned to our current distant emotional state.

Several weeks later, as we continued to attempt to address Samantha's experience of deprivation, fearfulness, and lack of enthusiasm, another song lyric came to my mind. This lyric was "a ship, a black freighter" which both Samantha and I had many rich associations to. The lyric came from "Pirate Jenny," a song from *The Threepenny Opera*, about a chambermaid, a "have not," who gets revenge on the "gentlemen" who have taken advantage of and abused her (Brecht & Weill, 1928). This song, like "Miss Otis Regrets," is about a woman who gets revenge, who does not remain passive and deprived but who takes pleasure in her ability to pay back those men who have hurt and demeaned her. It was as if my unconscious fantasies were continuing to press forward with the images of betrayal, abuse, and revenge that are the core themes in both "Miss Otis Regrets" and "Pirate Jenny."

As one of those surprises which happen frequently in analysis and are often thought of as projective identification, "Pirate Jenny" was one of Samantha's favorite songs; she knew it well and had many associations to it. In our joining together in singing and enacting this song, it became clear that we were both afraid of the implications of this song and of the passionate connection that returning to this transitional, symmetrical, symbolic mode of relating implied. The song brought us together in an excited way; we could both identify with "Pirate Jenny," and more importantly, Samantha could enjoy the murderous feelings that years of deprivation had left her with. I came to understand that it was me that Samantha would murder, that I was the disloyal lover, the arrogant, self-centered man in the songs "Miss Otis Regrets" and "Pirate Jenny." These songs felt less safe and required that we be willing to trust ourselves to the relationship and the process, to leave the safety of the known for the possible excitement of a new relationship.

The splitting that was symbolized and enacted through the songs of *Porgy and Bess* were transformed into active experiences of revenge, rage, and murder through the symmetrical symbolic enactment of "Pirate Jenny" and the images from *The Threepenny Opera*. These symbolic, symmetrical, transitional experiences allowed us to enter into a world in which the distinctions between analyst and patient, transference and countertransference disappeared, allowing us to symbolize and articulate both Samantha's and my own unconscious fantasies. These symmetrical experiences involved feelings of intense pleasure and desire as well as destruction and death, which were both exciting and frightening as we were drawn into the dream-like worlds of *Porgy and Bess*, "Pirate Jenny," and *The Threepenny Opera*.

I want to emphasize the importance of the experience of pleasure in these enactments which I believe are crucial aspects of the transformation of the patient's concrete, repetitive, externalized experiences into internal, symbolic, symmetrical experiences. Although not frequently articulated, pleasure is at the heart of Winnicott's (1971a) understanding of transitional experiences and his view of therapy as a subcategory of play, as well as Fonagy and colleagues' (2003, 2007) concept of the pretend mode, and Bruschweiler-Stern and colleagues' (BPCSG, 2007) description of the phenomenology of "now moments." Symmetrical interventions are often both pleasurable and frightening and require the analyst to abandon the safety of traditional, asymmetrical, declarative, interpretive approaches for symmetrical, symbolic moments of potential transformation and the opportunity to learn new implicit relational paradigms.

My use of songs reflects a symmetrical, symbolic approach to interpretation in which the analytic function moves beyond historical, linear explanations to ones which involve implicit, relational knowing, a process which occurs simultaneously on the nonverbal and verbal metaphorical level and as intersubjective enactments which incorporate pleasure in the transformational processes. The transformational models suggested by Winnicott's concept of transitional experience, Bion's concept of reverie and alpha function, Fonagy and colleagues' concept of mentalization, Lacan's concept of jouissance, and my concept of symmetrical symbolic experience all involve another mind, or subjectivity, in relation to the person's internal experience; these models are intersubjective and focus on the necessity for a deep awareness of what occurs inside the mind of the other. This paper suggests that it is not simply intersubjective relatedness that allows for the transformation of patients' concrete, externalized, disowned parts of the self, but that this intersubjective, symbolic experience must include experiences of pleasure in the implicit relational system of analyst and patient.

Like Freud's grandson, it is the pleasurable repetition which allows for the transformation and symbolization of concrete, frightening, evacuated experience to become incorporated through processes of mutual recognition (Benjamin, 1991) in pleasurable, intimate, intersubjective relationships such as that between mother and child or analyst and patient. I believe that the transitional experiences of *Porgy and Bess* and "Pirate Jenny" expressed Samantha's unconscious beliefs and fantasies that desire and pleasure were destructive. Like dreams and metaphors which organize experience in the unconscious, symmetrical, symbolic mode, these experiences in our analytic relationship allowed her to transform her phobic experiences of desire, pleasure, and negative view of herself as a woman into a new subjective, symbolic experience in which desire became a human possibility, delinked from its paralyzing relationship with the cultural and familial stereotypes of being deprived and destructive.

The transformational models discussed in this chapter are developmental and suggest that the analytic relationship facilitates more than the simple resolution of patient conflict and difficulty through insight or novel analytic experiences, but more importantly facilitates the development of capacity for mentalization and self-reflective thought (Fonagy et al., 2007), the capacity to dream (Bion, 1962; Ogden, 2007), to repair (Grotstein, 2000) or perhaps develop the dream screen, which allows patient to generate new, subjective meanings in their lives.

In thinking about my experiences with Samantha, I was reminded of Benjamin's (1991) discussion of the importance of the father's recognition of his daughter as a desiring subject and of the mutuality in the process of identification which we enacted in our playing *Porgy and Bess* and "Pirate Jenny." I want to underscore the importance of the analyst's use of symmetrical, symbolic interventions and the experience of enjoyment in the process of mutual identification, as well as the enactment of these unconscious fantasies as transitional experiences. However, it is also important to highlight the experience of danger that symmetrical moments of intense pleasure bring into the analytic playground; I believe that it is the apprehension of these dangers that often keeps us in the more restricted, interpretive, asymmetrical mode of interaction with patients. It is the fear of the danger of the loss of boundaries, as the analytic relationship moves into the metaphoric, dream-like, symmetrical, symbolic mode that keeps us from developing a transformational model of the psychoanalytic relationship.

NOTES

1. Sartre (Sartre & Camus, 2015) dramatically presents this dynamic of desire, jouissance, and vulnerability in his play "No Exit" where each person is both dependent on and terrified of an other's feelings about him/her.

2. Grotstein, Ogden, and Ferro are some of the theorists who describe this transformational view of the analytic relationship.

3. Following Bion's (1962) theory of thinking I use the concept of symbolic thought to represent thought which integrates affect perception and cognition into personal meaning. Ogden (2010) develops this idea in his paper Three Forms of Thinking.

4. Freud wrote A Child is Being Beaten in conjunction with his analysis of his daughter and interpreted these beating fantasies as reflecting Oedipal guilt. I would like to suggest that in these instances it represents women's disowned desire and an acknowledgment of being subordinated to men.

Chapter Six

Dissociative Processes as a Failure of Symbolic Functioning and Mentalization

The three previous chapters describe the use of transformational processes in psychoanalysis and psychotherapy. These approaches highlight the use of symmetrical, symbolic interpretive strategies in the development of a patient's capacity to move from the concrete, asymmetrical thought processes located in the external world to the capacity for mentalization, empathy, and understanding others' intentionality. Symmetrical, symbolic therapeutic strategies include the implicit procedural learning described by the BPCSG (2007) and right brain organized patterns of thought described by neuropsychologists (Schore, 2011). Psychoanalytic theorists make an important contribution to these converging views of transformational process by focusing on the necessity for the therapist to be able to use processes of reverie and affective elaboration of patients' concrete experience in a process which Bion (1965) described as the container contained, through which the patient or child can begin to develop their own capacity to think their own thoughts. The following three chapters address the analyst's and therapist's inability to think during sessions; a breakdown of the container contained function which leaves the analysts or therapist stuck in a world of concrete affective experiences flooded by bits of meaningless or frightening information and often watching the clock to see when the session will mercilessly end. Chapter 6 addresses working with patients who have experienced severe trauma and become lost in pathological dissociative experiences. Chapter 7 describes the breakdown in the container contained function in work with patients often categorized as borderline but who I would rather think of as in the autistic contiguous position (Ogden, 1989). Chapter 8 continues the discussion focusing on the supervisory relationship in which procedural learning seems to be a necessary aspect in the analyst's capacity to trust their own thoughts and not be fearful of being inadequate and feeling like a fool.

Understanding patients' disowned and dissociated experience and the contemporary interest in trauma has created a space for a deeper appreciation of Kleinian theory that emphasizes symbolization, countertransference, projective identification, enactment, and the importance of the analyst's immediate experience (Blass, 2011). Failure in the development of the capacity for symbolic thought is a consistent and critical element in dissociation and the ability to process trauma. In this chapter, I trace the evolution of the Kleinian concept of the development and failure of the capacity for symbolization, and how it relates to other contemporary psychoanalytic approaches with particular reference to trauma and dissociation. I suggest some clinical approaches which may facilitate the repair of the capacity for symbolic thought in patients who have experienced trauma and are in severe dissociative states.

Kleinian theory has two major dimensions: an interpersonal dimension, involving aggression, power and the structure of relationships; and a cognitive dimension, which describes the development of thinking from concrete organizations of experience as absolute facts, "truth," to symbolic experiences of personal meaning, reflection, empathy, possibility and hope. Both the interpersonal and intrapsychic dimensions are embedded in the paranoid-schizoid and depressive positions. In the depressive position the person can actively organize his/her experience in the world, as contrasted to the paranoid schizoid position in which the person is imprisoned, passively reacting to the push and pull of internal and external forces. Klein's (Ogden, 1992) thinking evolved from Freud's one person biological theory to a two person intersubjective approach, that focused on how meaning is generated and relationships structured. It is interesting to note the similarity between Klein's (1975a, 1975b) object relations theory and Sullivan's (1953) interpersonal theory of psychoanalysis. Each begins with the disorganizing experience of anxiety, emphasizes the importance of the interpersonal/familial context, the development of stages and positions, forms of knowing and strategies for anxiety avoidance. These similarities should not be surprising since both Klein and Sullivan were children of the twentieth century, deeply affected by the First and Second World Wars, and lived through a change from a culture which emphasized the production of goods to a culture which emphasized communication. Additionally, both theorists were deeply influenced by Ferenczi (1931), who unlike his peers, emphasized the importance of new experiences in the analytic relationship.

The interpersonal dimension of Kleinian theory involves greed, envy, destructiveness, and aggression, which was initially conceptualized as arising out of the death drive. Few contemporary Kleinians use the concept of the death drive; however, the emphasis on destructiveness, greed, and envy continues to be central to the paranoid-schizoid position and can be thought of as addressing the critical dimension of power and control: whether I control something or it controls me. The paranoid-schizoid position dominates the experiential world of people who have experienced trauma, where dissociation structures their experience of living in a timeless, concrete world of unchanging and repetitive traumatic experiences. The sense of powerlessness, masochistic forms of relatedness, lack of control, and being a thing in the world reflect experiences within the passive paranoid position,[1] while sadism, controlling forms of relatedness, hyper-responsibility, self-hate, blame, difficulties trusting or depending on others, and a sense of grandiosity reflect experiences within the active paranoid position. The recognition of one's destructiveness and limitations are the necessary precursors to the development of the depressive position and the capacity for symbolic thought, allowing for empathy and experiencing oneself and others as whole people, who have an internal world of feelings, wishes, intentions, and fantasies. People who have experienced trauma and are in dissociative states are unable to organize experience within the depressive position, where they could develop a sense of agency and an awareness of their own and others' internal experience.

These intrapsychic dimensions have a cognitive focus and describe two alternate ways of knowing the other. In the depressive position, the other is experienced as a whole person with an internal world of feelings, thoughts, and intentions, while in the paranoid-schizoid position, the other is experienced as a collection of part objects[2] existing only to provide services or supplies for an other person. Both positions represent the progressive development of symbolic processes, modes of creating meaning through the internalization of structures of relationship and meaning. These structures are similar to Bowlby's (1969) concept of working models, concepts of subjectivity (Stolorow, 2002; Stern, 1985), intersubjectivity (Benjamin, 2009; Ogden, 1994), and mentalization (Fonagy et al., 2003).

Kleinian therapists focus on how meaning is generated differently within the paranoid-schizoid and depressive positions. Subjective experience is never unmediated but always reflects a process through which experience is given both meaning and location. Segal (1978) suggests that the earliest form of thinking reflect a dual process of splitting, involving both affect and location; the earliest meaning is either good or bad and the earliest location is inside me or outside me. For example, the infant or child faced with the confusion and overwhelming stimulation that accompanies experiences of abuse attempts to separate his/her experience through splitting, first according to affect, good and bad, and then by location, inside me or outside me. The child can project or evacuate his/her experience into the other and as a result lives in a terrifying world of the passive paranoid position in which he/she is flooded by persecutory anxiety experiencing the other as bad. Alternatively, the person can evacuate the good feelings into the other, believing that if he/she were not bad, the other would be good and not need to punish him/her. In the first position, the passive paranoid-schizoid position, the individual feels like a victim in an unstable dangerous world. In the second approach, the active paranoid-schizoid position, the individual makes the world safe, while believing that he/she is in control, at fault, guilty, and ashamed. This second strategy, the active paranoid-schizoid position, is clinically more difficult because it negates the need for another while maintaining an internal nightmare world of horrible actions and feelings. This more grandiose strategy embraces Milton's (2007) famous phrase from *Paradise Lost*; "it is better to reign in Hell than serve in Heaven."

Bion and Winnicott extended Klein's concept of symbolic functioning, focusing on how the individual develops the capacity for symbolic thought within an intersubjective relationship with a parent or therapist. Winnicott's (1971a) concept of the development of transitional experience can be understood as an intersubjective process, in which the child gives an object (i.e. a doll or toy) a personal meaning which is accepted and elaborated by the parent and family, who acknowledge the child's ability to create symbolic experience through giving meaning and a physical place to an object, which is then experienced as having the quality of being alive, as when a child insists that the family pay attention to "my baby," or to an imaginary companion. Children who have been in severely abusive families often lack the experience of affirmation and being recognized as one who can create meaning through the development of transitional objects and experiences. Rather they experience the opposite response from their parents and are told what they experience is false and that their mother or father becomes a threatening, persecutory presence telling them that they will be hurt or killed if they talk about their experience.

Winnicott's development of the concept of transitional experience is a radical two person approach to the creation of meaning, which requires a safe, playful relationship with a parent, caretaker, or therapist. Winnicott's (1971a) concept of transitional experience is an elaboration of the squiggle game (Winnicott, 1958; Soni, 2012) and the basis of his approach to psychoanalytic treatment which emphasized the mutual creation of subjective meaning. For Winnicott, the creation of meaning is an intersubjective process located in an evolving third domain[3] of experience separate from purely internal experience and purely objective experience. Winnicott describes this domain of meaning making as a transitional space, an intersubjective domain where play, art, religion, personal values, and meanings develop. For Winnicott, transitional space differs from the purely objective space of the external world of facts, authority, and rules, which he sees as being imposed on the child in a series of impingements, and which results in the development of an objective, false self, a not-me organization of experience.

Winnicott, like others who have been influenced by Klein, suggests that the development of knowledge or meaning occurs differently in the external world of facts and work as contrasted with the intersubjective world of personal relationships, intimacy, and play. Recognition of an objective and a subjective world of meaning is important in understanding people who have experienced trauma and dissociation because trauma and dissociation disrupt the development of intersubjective transitional space while often allowing a person to function reasonably well in the operational world of facts, rules, and authority. These patients are often able to function competently in the external world of facts but are unable to function in the intersubjective world of meanings, intimacy, and play; alternatively they may be unable to differentiate these two realms and experience confusion between the subjective world of meanings and the external world of facts.

In parallel to Winnicott, Bion (1959, 1962) developed an intersubjective theory of creating meaning, of thinking. However, where Winnicott described a spontaneous, experience-near process, initiated by the child and responded to by the parent, Bion described a theoretical system of projective and introjective identification through which the child comes to terms with painful experiences. Bion starts with the premise that the child cannot tolerate, think about, or contain his/her painful experiences in an immature mind, and so must be evacuated or projected into a parent or caretaking other who would possibly be able to contain and think about these painful experiences. Bion elaborates Klein's (Ogden, 1992) concept of projective identification, reconceptualizing it as an explicitly two person intersubjective process in which the parent, or a therapist, can accept, contain, affectively and symbolically elaborate the child's anxiety filled projections. Bion referred to this process of affective and symbolic elaboration of projected or evacuated experience in different terms as he developed his theory of thinking, including the concepts of alpha function, reverie, and night and awake dreaming. In a healthy situation, the parent or other is able to contain and tolerate the anxiety and destructiveness of the child's projections and elaborate them into meaningful, less concrete, less anxiety filled experiences which the child can internalize and experience as thought. However, miscarriages of this process of creating symbols, creating meaning, occur when the parent or therapist cannot contain (tolerate) the child's projection and instead rejects the projective experience and blames or accuses the child as being bad or at fault. This inability to contain and affectively elaborate projected experience often results in pathological projective identification, leading to a tragic game of "hot potato" in which the projected disowned experience continues to cycle between parent and child, becoming reified as an external fact, a fixed, concrete action, rather than a thought or symbolic experience.

Pathological projective identification occurs when a parent or therapist is unable to contain and symbolically elaborate the child's or patient's experience, becoming anxious, distraught, distracted, sleepy, unable to think, attacking or blaming the child or patient for bringing unmanageable experiences into their world. Patients who have been sexually abused by family members describe how when they were finally able to tell another family member, often their mother, about the experience of sexual abuse, their words were angrily rejected, and they were told that it did not happen, that it should never be talked about, and that they are bad, a liar, and at fault. Because these experiences were not contained and therefore could not be thought about and elaborated, they remain concrete, unthinkable experiences, which are dissociated and repeatedly enacted and re-experienced in new relationships as real events, perceptions, and facts in the external world. For people who have experienced trauma and PTSD their flashbacks and intrusive thoughts often occur in which the images or actual experiences (perceptions) recur and are felt as if they are real events occurring in the present and not memories of the past or involving reflective thought processes. These PTSD experiences reflect unprocessed experiences, protoemotional and protosensory (Ferro, 2006) experiences which have not been contained and exist as a "thing in itself," as an evacuated, concrete, external experience and not as an internal experience or memory.

CASE ILLUSTRATION OF THE INABILITY TO CONTAIN TRAUMATIC EXPERIENCE

Let me illustrate the complex process of the inability to contain traumatic experience and the resulting failures of symbolization in a case in which the patient had profound sexual trauma and lived in a world in which she was in dissociated states a great deal of the time, as well as in states of constant terror and anxiety. I was supervising an experienced psychoanalytic therapist who had difficulty talking about this case because she experienced a great deal of shame and was, for her, unusually afraid of being criticized for failing to help her patient. She was also ashamed that she was barely able to stay awake in her sessions. This therapist's experience is not unusual when working with extremely traumatized patients, where the capacity to symbolize, to contain, and to affectively elaborate either your own or the patient's experience completely collapses. Bion (1959) described periods of being unable to think as attacks on linking, a collapse of the container-contained function in the therapist, who becomes completely and concretely identified with the patient's disowned and evacuated feelings. We see in this collapse of the therapist's capacity to symbolize (Shoenhals, 1996) a movement into the paranoid-schizoid position, with the development of severe persecutory anxiety and symbolic equations where thought and action are experienced as identical, as when this therapist believed that she is a "bad" person who should be shunned by me in supervision. This description is like that of Fonagy et al.'s (2003) description of states of extreme psychic equivalence, where what is in my mind is in the world and also in the other's mind.

The collapse of the capacity to symbolize occurred in both the therapeutic relationship and the supervisory relationship. I also felt deeply ashamed and had avoided my own awareness that I also became sleepy and distracted in our supervisory sessions and that I felt ashamed and that I was a "bad" supervisor. Experiences of sleepiness and distraction often occur when working with dissociative patients in the therapist and supervisor as the containing function becomes too painful. It is interesting to think of the supervisory relationship as a part of a larger system comprised of the patient, therapist, and supervisor all of whom are attempting to process the dissociated experiences. In this situation no member of this supervision system was able to function in a symbolic way; each of us, patient, therapist, and supervisor, experienced ourselves in paranoid-schizoid states of persecutory anxiety, experiencing our worlds in modes of symbolic equivalence, dominated by action and concrete beliefs. Rather than being able to contain, elaborate, and symbolize, we became disconnected, helpless, fearful, and useless part objects.

Supervision is often a very important adjunct for the therapist when working with extremely traumatized patients; it has the potential of becoming a safe place where the therapist and supervisor can begin to contain and elaborate the inevitable parallel experiences of dissociation in the overlapping dyads of patient and therapist and therapist and supervisor. The turning point in my relationship with this therapist occurred when I, as the supervisor, was able to articulate my shameful feelings of boredom, disinterest, and sleepiness, saying that I felt like a bad supervisor—not doing my job. My acknowledgment, my beginning attempts to articulate and inhabit and play with these experiences, rather than deny and disown the experience of being "bad," opened up a transitional space in the supervision where both myself and the therapist were able to begin to play with the experiences of being a "bad" supervisor and a "bad" therapist. Being able to contain, articulate, and symbolize projected and dissociated experience of badness is a crucial step in moving from paranoid-schizoid states of persecutory anxiety and symbolic or psychic equivalence to depressive, symbolic experiences, including those of empathy and compassion. Our capacity to symbolize in supervision, to play with various experiences, resulted in the therapist becoming able to be more present in the therapy dyad and to begin to contain and articulate the horrible incestuous experiences that her patient reported, and the resulting nightmare experiences which flooded both her conscious and unconscious worlds.

This patient had horrible incestuous experiences which continued from childhood through adolescence. Each night her father would come into the room that she shared with her sister and sexually abuse her sister while she would pretend to be asleep, attempting to dissociate the sounds, smells, and sights of her father's attacks on her older sister.

In therapy the patient reported the following deeply disturbing experiences: being flooded by intense, painful, somatic experiences; being terrified every night believing that she was being spied upon; worried that she would be trapped in a fire in her apartment and constantly feeling that she was in danger of being sexually assaulted on the streets and at work. She experienced and described all of this as if she was describing absolute truth, the facts of her existence; she often talked about suicide as the only possible escape. It is hard to describe how intense these experiences were and how intensely it affected the therapist, who believed that she was not being helpful becoming sleepy and distracted. When the patient would miss appointments, the therapist felt intense panic and concern that something had happened to her; she feared and had images in which her patient had been raped, or had committed suicide. In addition to being unable to contain and elaborate the patient's incestuous experiences, the therapist also felt extremely guilty and filled with shame when she would think about how much better her life was than her patient's. The patient's symptoms and the therapist's experiences of dissociation, shame, and guilt were concrete representations, symbolic equivalents, of the uncontained, unelaborated and unsymbolized derivatives of the patient's evacuated experience. Because these experiences were not symbolized, they felt absolutely real. Often the patient experienced these symbolic equivalents as positive hallucinations (men watching her in her room), which alternated with her sleepy absences, her dissociative experiences, which can be thought of as negative hallucinations.

Slowly supervision took on the quality of a transitional experience. We became able to contain and elaborate some of the therapist's and supervisor's feelings as concrete proto-emotional symbolic experiences; for example, our sleepy and shameful dissociation, we thought of as a feeling that it would be better to be dead then to be lying in bed while your sister is repeatedly raped by your father. The patient's belief that she was being spied on, that her room was on fire, and her painful somatic experiences all represented concrete representations of the uncontained and unsymbolized experiences of her childhood. Perhaps the most difficult work had to do with the therapist recognizing her guilt over thinking that her life was much better than the patient's. Symbolizing her guilt represented an unacceptable thought for the therapist, who was committed to being compassionate toward her patient. However, as we attempted to tolerate and affectively elaborate this image, playing with her guilt feelings, it became clear that this unacceptable thought also represented the patient's intolerable thoughts as she witnessed her sister being repeatedly raped and probably felt glad that it was not her.[4] Related to this complex set of thoughts about guilt, which became quite difficult, was the process of the therapist recognizing and working with the patient's envy, sexual desires, and destructiveness toward her and her life. The patient was in a process of moving from the passive paranoid position of being a victim to the active paranoid position of being aggressive and angry which was understandably difficult to contain. The work of containing, affectively elaborating, and symbolizing these experiences did not happen very quickly; not only were these experiences difficult to contain, elaborate, and symbolize, but the therapeutic work went well beyond asymmetrical interpretation, explaining the patient's symptoms in relation to her developmental history. Therapy involved having to live through, inhabit, and play in the horrific transitional space which this patient brought into therapy.[5] Therapy for many patients involves the development of presentational rather than discursive symbols, in a situation that is more like a theater than a laboratory. Along with processes of progressive symbolization, and playfully enacting these transitional experiences, the patient began to develop her own capacity to symbolize, to contain, and to affectively elaborate experience which previously had been extremely limited because of her history of trauma.

Both Bion and Winnicott describe the capacity for symbolic experience as a developmental achievement which occurs differently in the world of subjective experience and the world of objective experience. Matte-Blanco's (1975) and Newirth'a (2003) bi-logical theory of thinking described the functions and structure in thinking about the external world of objects, asymmetrical thought, and thinking about emotional, intimate, and intersubjective thought, symmetrical thinking. Symmetry and asymmetry are different forms of creating meaning, of symbolization, in which the same experience may take on very different meanings. Matte-Blanco (1988) suggests that experiences which are the result of pathological projective identification, such as in families or situations in which traumatic events remain uncontained and unelaborated by an other (parent or therapist) are experienced asymmetrically as facts, as immutable events in the objective world which cannot be changed. Bion's concepts of alpha function, reverie, and dream-work are symmetrical processes of affective and symbolic elaboration in which the therapist's identifications and experiences of similarities are an initial step in elaborating the patient's dissociated experience. For example, the patient that we are discussing hallucinated people spying on her as a fact. She could not understand that this was an internal experience which reflected her experience of watching her sister being raped and an awareness that her father enjoyed watching her being tortured, tormented, and trapped in this unbearable situation. In supervision we slowly recognized that both the therapist and supervisor also experienced themselves as being trapped and tortured, and had to contain and elaborate this horrific unconscious symmetrization, the dedifferentiation (identification) of each of us with the patient. The therapist had to become able to inhabit this space, creating a transitional experience and affectively elaborating her terrible thoughts, including the thought that she was glad that her life was not as horrible as the patient's. This is a process of symmetrization, a dedifferentiation, and eventual playful elaboration of concrete asymmetrical experiences which became symbolized in the safety of the transitional space created within the supervisory and therapeutic relationships.

Matte-Blanco's bi-logical theory and Fonagy's and Target's (1996; 2000) concept of mentalization[6] are similar approaches to the development of the concept of symbolization. Fonagy et al., conceptualize two separate modes of representing experience, the mode of psychic equivalence and the pretend mode, and suggest that trauma interferes with the integration of these two primary modes of representation into the capacity for mentalization. Fonagy and Target (2000, p. 853) suggest that this "failure to mentalise adequately is compounded by the persistence of an undifferentiated mode of representing external and internal experience. This is rooted in a childlike understanding of mental states in which feelings and ideas are construed as direct (or equivalent) representations of reality with consequent exaggeration of their importance and extension of their implications. This mode of functioning tends to be self-perpetuating. The experience of unconscious as well as conscious feelings and ideas as equivalent to physical reality inhibits the individual's capacity to suspend the immediacy of their experience and to create the psychological space to 'play with reality'" which is common to people who have experienced trauma and dissociate.

Failure in the development of mentalization arises out of a mother's failure to contain and articulate the child's affective experience in a "marked," affective, playful, ironic, exaggerated, and less frightening way. The mother's or caretaker's ability to contain and elaborate experience in "marked" way allows the child to recognize that the mother is mirroring the child's frightening experience in a safer, second order or symbolic form which allows the child to internalize this experience as something to be thought about in a less fearful way. If this capacity for marked, playful mirroring (transitional space) does not occur, the child internalizes the experience concretely as the mother's experience, as an external reality, a fact which may be experienced as an alien object or voice occurring internally but having the character of an external event organized asymmetrically. A traumatized child unable to experience the mother or therapist as a safe person capable of containing and symmetrically elaborating their experience will tend to withdraw into the pretend mode, which becomes the basis for dissociation, creating an isolated paranoid world which may be more adaptive then being in the actual eternal world. In contrast to this withdrawal into unitary and dissociative play or fantasy, Fonagy and Target (2000) describe the importance of being able to play with others as the bridge which integrates the pretend mode and the mode of psychic equivalence and leads to the development of the capacity for mentalization, the ability to take different perspectives, to understand motivational and intentional states, and to create meaning in relationships.

Although Fonagy does not define himself as a "Kleinian," his theoretical and clinical work has been heavily influenced by Bion and Winnicott. His clinical work focuses on the capacity to create meaning, emphasizing the use of countertransference, the therapist's ability to overcome the pressure to dissociate, to be able to symbolize, and maintain an intersubjective awareness of the patient as a whole person. In describing the therapeutic experience, Fonagy and Target (2000, p. 859) state: "The countertransference response is often a sense of emptiness, which we see as the result of an attempt to reduce both people to an equally unthinking state . . ." Fonagy and Target (2000, p. 868) suggest that: "The focus of technique in such cases is thus no longer making conscious what was unconscious. We believe an appropriate technical priority is the survival of the analyst's picture of the patient's mental state in his mind." It is important to recognize that this is a process that takes time as the therapist is able to move from a dissociated state, unable to think, to one which often begins with seemingly odd personal experiences, such as feelings of shame or guilt, and becomes, through states of reverie, meaningful experiences in the transference countertransference relationship.

This emphasis on countertransference, including the inevitability of dissociation and the importance of recovering the intersubjective ability to contain and affectively elaborate the experience of the patient as a subject, and to generate symbolic meaning, is at the core of Kleinian technique. The "here and now" (Blass, 2011), moment to moment experience is extremely important in working with traumatized and dissociative patients where the therapist almost always finds him/herself in dissociative states, unable to think, inhabiting paranoid-schizoid states of self-hatred and inadequacy. These countertransference experiences reflect a collapse of the container-contained function, resulting in concrete symmetrical identifications with the patient and the patient's projections. This inevitable collapse of the container-contained function requires a great deal of work by the therapist and supervisor to repair their capacity for reverie, to be able to affectively and symmetrically elaborate their own and their patients' experiences.

Following Bion, Ogden (2003) describes this process of containing and affectively elaborating symmetrical experience as becoming able to dream the patient into existence, which he emphasizes may take a long time to achieve while the analyst himself is in a distracted, dissociated state. It is very important for the therapist to be able to utilize symmetrical forms of thinking, including associations to similar personal experiences, uncomfortable fantasies, songs, and humorous thoughts which help create a playful, transitional space. As the therapist is able to subjectively play with these experiences, it will allow the treatment to move toward a transitional space which will allow the patient to develop the capacity for symbolic thought, to mentalize their past experiences, and to know others as whole persons who have separate internal experiences. Chapter 7 continues to develop the concept of the broken container, the inability to function symbolically with patients who are unable to symbolize or mentalize their experience while chapter 8 focuses on the way supervision can be of use in developing the containing function and the patients' capacity for symbolic thought.

NOTES

1. See Newirth (2003) for a more extensive discussion of the passive and active paranoid-schizoid position.
2. The use of people as part objects includes exploiting individuals as sexual objects, the use of individuals for particular functions, and the lack of recognition of an inner life of feelings, beliefs, and thoughts.
3. Ogden's (1994) and Benjamin's (2009) concepts of the third are developments of Winnicott's concept of transitional experience and describe an intersubjective perspective on the mutual development of meaning.
4. This seems to be an example of survivor's guilt.
5. See Davies and Frawley (1992) for more examples of the difficulty of working with patients who have been sexually abused.
6. Fonagy et al.'s use of the concept of mentalization parallels the Kleinian concept of symbolization. His work seems to reflect an integration of Kleinian object relations theory and developmental research. We will use mentalization and symbolization as highly related concepts arising within overlapping areas of psychoanalysis and developmental psychology.

Chapter Seven

The Broken Container: Developing Symbolic Processes in Psychotherapy

In *'Wild' Psycho-Analysis*, Freud (1910, p. 226) describes a patient who was shattered by her young analyst's interpretation that her lack of sexual relations with her husband was the cause of her psychological problems. Freud criticized this therapist, and suggested that this kind of *'Wild' Psycho-Analysis* occurs when interpretations are made prematurely, before a patient has "reached the neighborhood of what has been repressed," or has developed "a sufficient attachment, transference, to the physician for his[1] emotional relationship to him to make a fresh flight impossible." Contemporary relational and Kleinian psychoanalysis has expanded Freud's emphasis on the transference relationship, defining transference as the total situation (Joseph, 1985), a mutual relationship (Aron, 1990; Renik, 1995; Benjamin, 2009) as providing potentially new experiences and that the analyst function as a container (Bion, 1970; Ogden, 2010), using processes of reverie to experience, affectively elaborate, and develop the patient's concrete projective identifications into symbolic experiences which can be reinternalized through interpretations centered on the transference countertransference relationship. This chapter will present a contemporary perspective on *'Wild' Psycho-Analysis*, one in which the analyst and not the patient becomes shattered by premature, overwhelming, affective experiences within the transference countertransference relationship.

Bion's concept of the container contained relationship has been extremely useful as a metaphor for the contemporary understanding of therapeutic action within the transference countertransference relationship and as an algorithm for the development of the capacity for symbolic thought. As a metaphor it describes the intense affective experiences of the analyst in the process of attempting to tolerate and symbolize the patient's evacuated, concrete experience. Like much of the psychoanalytic literature, this metaphor is typically described in somewhat heroic terms in which the analyst through the use of reverie succeeds in accepting, making meaning, and interpreting his/her patient's disowned experience. However, Bion's idea of the container contained is more than a metaphor, it is a description of a complex set of intersubjective processes, an algorithm in which meaninglessness, and the destruction of the capacity to think and believe in one's own ability to be a therapist, often collapses. The container, the analyst's mind, becomes broken; we are unable to think and make meaning and have to redevelop our own capacity to contain and symbolize experience within the countertransference transference relationship.

This chapter will present two cases, which were written by members of a supervision group and presented (Newirth, 2010) at the Division 39 Conference in 2010. I am very grateful to Kristin Reale (2010) and Meredith Darcy (2010) for their generosity, courage, and openness in presenting their clinical work and including it in this chapter. These two cases were written largely from the analyst's perspective, in which each therapist became dislodged from her usual role as a helpful therapist and experienced a breakdown in the capacity to think, to be present, to understand the transference countertransference relationship, and to use reverie to elaborate affect and meaning. In these therapy relationships, the analysts were overwhelmed by the intensity and concreteness of the affects generated in the transference countertransference relationships, feeling that their usual capacity to contain affects, enactments, and fantasy had become shattered and were only able to cling to a desperate hope that the overwhelming shameful experiences of rage, revulsion, and raunchiness would remain secret. These analysts experienced themselves in the midst of truly wild analyses. From a diagnostic perspective, these patients may be thought of as in the autistic contiguous position (Ogden, 1989) or as borderline personality disorders (Fonagy et al., 2003). For each patient there had been many early failures in the holding environment, in integrating the pretend mode and the mode of psychic equivalence, and these patients are unable to regulate emotions other than through action, cannot mentalize or symbolize their experience.

Ogden (1995) presents many interesting illustrations of the analyst's inability to contain patients' pathological projective identifications. He describes distracted states in which out of his awareness he experienced concrete signs of his patient's projective identifications, often finding himself disconnected and dominated by unbidden thoughts or actions, which eventually through processes of self-reflection, personal associations, and reverie he affectively elaborates and develops these transformed rudimentary thoughts into symbolic or metaphoric experiences of his relationship with the patient. In a particularly striking example, he (Ogden, 1995) finds himself repeatedly, and outside of his awareness, taking his pulse. As time goes by and he begins to recognize these actions as implicitly meaningful, he becomes curious and reflects on both the concreteness and oddness of his behavior, and through personal associations and reverie, he symbolizes the unconscious experience that this patient evacuated into him, which he understood as a question, a metaphor of whether she could tolerate being alive or must continue her existence in a state of deadness.

The two cases that will be discussed in this chapter describe situations in which there is a breakdown of the containing function, the analysts became unable to think, were overwhelmed by intolerable and unacceptable affects, unable to function in either the two person mode as a container for the patient's projections, or in the one person mode, able to reflect on, associate to, or use imaginative process of reverie to generate the meaning encapsulated in their transference countertransference experience. In these situations both analysts felt filled with shame, often simply wanting to flee from feelings of being trapped, feeling that they have lost their connection to their professional community, their identity, and their capacity to think. We became curious about these situations in which there is a breakdown of the analyst's containing function. Does the breakdown in the container contained process simply reflect personal countertransference issue, does it reflect some basic fault in the patient which limits his or her ability to be analyzed, or is it an enactment of core, painful moments in the patient's life that are being relived in the analysis, in order to facilitate the development of the patient's capacity to think and use symbolic, self-reflective process.

Both the one person and two person concepts of the container contained describe thinking as a three dimensional process, involving self-reflective, playful, imaginative process of reverie, similar to Fonagy's and Target's (1996) concept of mentalization. Segal (1978) believes that symbolic thought involves the experience of possibility rather than certainty, and Winnicott's theory of transitional experience is an expansion of the Kleininan theory of symbolization which emphasizes the capacity for play and the creation of intersubjective meaning. However, when the containing function breaks down in an analytic relationship, we experience ourselves in a concrete two dimensional world, either terrifyingly fused with our patient's experiences and thoughts (psychic or symbolic equivalents), or absolutely alone, filled with shame, floating in formless space, cut off from human contact. We have come to understand the experience of the breakdown of the container contained function as a return to the autistic contiguous position (Ogden, 1989; Tustin, 1980) in which both analyst and patient are trapped, in desperate, shameful moments of overwhelming affects, body experiences, and sensory over stimulation.

The following clinical examples were provided by Kristin Reale (2010) and Meredith Darcy (2010) who were members of a small ongoing supervision group that attempted to function as a container as the analysts felt that their ability to contain their patients' autistic experiences and thoughts completely broke down. The supervision group attempted to operate as a container, facilitating each analyst's ability to regain her balance and begin to think and symbolize her experiences. Often in supervision we experienced ourselves being flooded by the concreteness of the analyst's experience of the therapy, becoming unable to think, experiencing a rupture in the containing function of the group, as we felt ourselves in states of confusion, ignorance, and shame. Often we would begin to make jokes about ourselves, the treatment and the patient; feeling more like we were on Saturday Night Live than in a serious psychoanalytic situation. Primitive humor and jokes often seemed like the first form of symbolization that we could begin to use, which allowed us to both enact the situation and stand back and think, feeling safe in the warmth of our relationship and recognizing the absurdity of the work of analysis. From these humorous experiences we were able to develop the ability to contain the therapist's and patient's anguish and develop a greater sense of understanding and possible symmetrical symbolic interventions that would be useful in the analytic relationship.

Both patients suffered from early developmental disasters with parental availability and lacked caretakers who had the capacity to contain painful thoughts and be empathic with their child which resulted in their inability to develop beyond the autistic contiguous position. Each patient seemed to experience relationships two dimensionally, either fused with an other or totally isolated. The content of the sessions often reflected the autistic contiguous position (Ogden, 1989), focusing on fused connections with others defining the physical limits and body boundaries, through aggression, sexual, oral, and anal bodily functions. We have come to understand the breakdown of the analytic container contained function, and the overwhelming shameful affects experienced by the analyst, as an enactment and re-creation of the failed intersubjective relationship of the parental container contained relationship and the floods of unmodulated affect and sensory experiences which defined each patient's early experiences of isolation and fusion in the autistic contiguous position. I suggest that the reader try to experience him/her self as the analyst in these cases, to have a first person experience of the breakdown and reconstitution of the psychoanalytic containing function.

DAVID[2]

David had just woken up from a ten minute "nap" on my couch, legs stretched out feet dangling over the edge, the couch being too short for what he is seeking. During these often taken naps he reminds me of a baby and a teenager all mixed into one. I had watched him slowly doze off in a peaceful state minutes before as I posed the question to myself again: is he sleeping to block me out or to "take me in"? I sometimes find him disappearing into my couch, eyelids heavy, just as I am relaying a beautifully crafted "perfectly correct" interpretation. It has occurred to me that my interpretations may just be a lullaby for him—mama putting him to sleep. As he startles back awake, he smirks, repositions his yarmulke and tells me again how this is the *best* place for him, how much he *loves* me and how "*sweet*" I am. These quiet, calm naps occur in the midst of unpredictably chaotic sessions with David, usually after he has shown up at least 30 minutes late for his weekly double session. Minutes after waking he is usually yelling at a client or commanding a driver on his cell phone, one of at least five calls he answers or makes during our sessions. He erratically slips into different languages on these calls . . . English, Russian, Hebrew. Sometimes the calls are for his thriving business, other times they are calls with his wife. He winks at me as he takes his calls, blows me a kiss as he mouths "sorry." I meekly grin and nod, completely annoyed feeling that he treats me like one of his inferior gentile mistresses, here for the taking. These phone calls drive me crazy; I feel enraged that he doesn't see how disruptive it is to "our work." As I wait for him, I wonder if it is his unconscious intention to drive me crazy. I feel angry with him for "disrespecting my time and space" and not talking about "what he needs to." These moments reflect the breakdown of the containing function, the patient's inability to recognize the presence of another and the therapist decision to attempt to intersubjectively address the patient's lack of boundaries as contrasted with an attempt to instantiate traditional analytic rules and boundaries.

I suppress the urge to make a declaration of the "no phone calls in session" policy. My fruitless prior attempts at making such rules and regulations have made me feel much less like a therapist establishing valuable boundaries and more like a naïve mother trying to grasp for control of her wild two year old. After he abruptly ends the call, I try to process with him what his phone calls mean during session, his lateness, and how this may point to his avoidance of feelings about our relationship. I believe that if I rationally interpret these enactments, we could work them through. But these efforts feel dead and robotic and most often lead to him asking me why he can't just "have what he wants," meaning a sexual relationship with me, inviting me onto the couch with him. He is only half-kidding. I usually fumble in my professional response to him.

I often feel annoyed with him for not following "the rules" of therapy, although I know theoretically why: he comes from a world of rules by which he has felt confined and controlled. David is an orthodox Jew in his mid-thirties with one foot deep into the culture and religion with the other foot hanging overboard. He was one of eleven children and speaks of a childhood where he never felt anything like love, was not held or spoken with, and questions his own ability to ever love. While I am feeling frustrated with him, at my most emotionally separate times I imagine that deep underneath he is feeling petrified, afraid of my attempts to connect with him, a relationship that he so desperately wants but must strike terror for him deep within. I know until I fully understand these enactments between us I will feel lost and locked in a battle of control with him. Unlike when I am with my other patients, when I am with David I feel like a therapist "winging it," barely holding on to any boundary that all my graduate professors would have made seem essential to "good proper treatment."

When I first began treating David he was struggling with a gambling addiction, spending his nights until 3:00 or 4:00 in the morning in dimly lit dangerous New York City basements betting thousands of dollars on poker games. He relayed how more than once the men playing alongside him would use their weapons to threaten one another. Other times, masked gangsters would break into the basement, guns pulled demanding everyone's money. He was obviously *thrilled* by all of this. He loved that he was the "crazy Orthodox" sitting amongst this crowd. He loved the danger, the money, the power, how they just "didn't know what to do with him." Boy, I could relate to this feeling! I had worked with addicts for years early in my training. I knew very well their deep attachment to the substance . . . the heroin, the alcohol, the gambling, the deep desire for mother love. These attachments were as strong as the drugged feeling of your very first kiss. And I knew that his needs would ultimately require a shift from gambling to a live human being, a being with feeling, if all went well. I knew this was me. And this felt like too much to hold for one person! I find myself swaying between wanting to be there for him always, and wanting to run.

In the beginning of his treatment he had hidden sexual relationships with many women—all outside of his Orthodox culture. They were very secret . . . all behind closed doors, all sounded wild and otherworldly. Most of the women were from South American countries. I imagined them with olive skin and thick accents. He described holding them down while having sex with them, wanting them to tell him how much they want him, need him. He says he only experiences sexual satisfaction when he is "on top" dominating them, controlling the sex, making them cry out for him. He often states how much he "just hates" Jewish women, "they all want a man to give and give to them while giving nothing of themselves." He feels so deprived by them while underneath he craves so much attention. At the beginning of treatment, he would tell me he "picked me" because I, too, like his mistresses, was an "outsider" and would keep his secrets. David often comments on my physical appearance, sometimes complimenting me, other times criticizing me with a devious smile, telling me how I should wear my hair, what clothes or jewelry would "look better" on me, etc. His comments throw me off balance, and again have me grasping for some therapeutic framework that I can rely on. These remarks feel like jabs, making me feel anxious and irritated. I sometimes ruminate about him, having swirling thoughts how I must find some way to "use" my anger like all the good theorists say, that his sessions can't possibly go on like this.

It was over six months of treatment before I felt any tinge of annoyance at David's neediness, chaotic ways, demands of me, or his attempts at seducing or controlling me and our sessions. And now more than two years into his treatment I find myself not looking forward to seeing him like I used to. I feel exhausted with having to manage my reactions to his provocative ways; I am less and less spontaneous with him and more bogged down in the chaotic transference countertransference relationship. I spend time before sessions anticipating how I will ward off his sexual advances and chaotic behavior, while somehow staying in the analytic framework and feeling useful to him. This moment seems to reflect a shift in the transference countertransference situation as the therapist gives up thoughts of the containing function while feeling that all she can do is survive the next set of assaults from the patient. Few therapists are willing to acknowledge this experience of breakdown and desperation.

Being with David I vacillate between feeling a sense of deep empathy with his emotional isolation and feeling absolutely devoured by him. When consumed, I experience an evacuation of feeling and thought . . . I CAN'T think and it's like I can only feel CAGED . This is sometimes followed by a fleeting feeling of terror, maybe I should be more afraid of David; that there is something more dangerous about him that I am not letting myself be aware of. Would he stalk me? During these pangs of terror, my mind travels back to our very first session. He said that he shouldn't carry a gun because he doesn't trust himself with it; how he is too impulsive, has intense road rage and such. This is a part of him I have never seen. But I am realizing now that my fear is related to how incredibly *out of control* he feels, and how much of this is "put into me." After the fright, I can usually settle back into the here and now, away from my far away, yet intuitive, thoughts, and back to "the session." And I once again feel empathy for him, and I begin again to enjoy his humor; always very bright and witty, always with a double meaning. While his wit reflects his awareness of his emotional detachment out in his world, it also feels like a loud warning signal blaring that we have hit our limit of intimacy.

During my "dreams" in session with him I truly see him riding a wave. I see an image of David surfing massive waves and being slammed around. And then miraculously he perfectly catches the next wave. This next wave is the $20,000 he brought in last night while "his boy" bet on games for him in Vegas. And seeing him catch the curl of that monster wave and ride it gently down, I think, "Man he's got it made." And then, I become more consciously present, I hear his breathing, hear his foot tapping, see how unkempt he is in front of me. And then again I have returned to my reverie: I see him barely holding on to his board in calm water with the next mammoth wave right behind him. Thing is, he might not see this one in time to get back on his feet again. But he most always does.

Within the first two years of treatment a lot happened: I got married, he got married, I got pregnant, his wife lost a baby. I felt as if he was mirroring my life, waiting for my next move. In the weeks leading up to my maternity leave (where I planned to be away for four months), David returned to gambling—a lot of gambling. He had initially "kicked" the gambling addiction five months into treatment. I felt that somehow I had to "catch" this before I was to go on maternity leave. But he felt far gone, and I felt huge. I knew there was so much happening between us . . . our relationship felt swirling to me, out of control, fast. I couldn't keep up. My baby inside of me would twist and turn and kick me hard while I sat with David. I thought of how he was one of eleven children—smack dab in the middle. Just like my caseload. I would get so overwhelmed in session with him just thinking about my impending leave. How could I possibly give enough to each patient when there were two dozen of them. I remember clearly that in my reverie, I felt what it was like for him to be one of so many children. This is when I told David that it wasn't that he was just the sixth of eleven children . . . it was like he was "number 45." He looked up smiling from ear to ear, and said, "No, no. I wasn't just 45. I was 45-B." We laughed. I had gotten his sense of floating in a sea of children. Lost, alone, no anchor. And here I was trying to find someway to anchor him while I went off to take care of the "next one" . . . my own baby.

He couldn't talk of my leaving—he just thought I made such a big deal about things. I'd say that I was concerned about how he'd feel with my being gone, and how I think it would be best if we talked about it and maybe planned for phone sessions. He'd shoot this down immediately. His anxiety was really on the rise, his breathing was rapid and with a tick, and he had returned to much of his sexual and monetary compulsivity. But he'd say, "What's a couple weeks?! I'll be fine!!" Irritated by his minimization of my having a baby and returning to work, I reminded him more than once that it was four *months*, ***not*** a couple weeks. I learned quickly that when it came to me being outside this room with him, he just *didn't want to know*. What I also learned was that I had to let him go, drift out to sea. It was where he was comfortable right now. I had done my best to give him a life jacket while I was gone. I felt that he had the jacket in hand . . . it was right there—I was right there—just a phone call away—but he wouldn't fasten it. I knew he'd unravel, and he did.

David often speaks of his of his wife and her clinginess which he resents, how he thinks of calling many of his recent secret non-Jewish girlfriends for sex in hotels—and then rambles back to how perfect his wife is for him. He speaks of her miscarriage and her desire for another pregnancy with a flippant arrogant tone, hoping that a baby will "get her off his back," "keep her busy." He tells me *all* men think like this, that no man really wants to be married, and asks if I am concerned that my husband feels the same way. I dodge his questions, feel insecure and soon enough enraged with what I can only see at the time: his masochistic male chauvinist ways. David most always hides *his own* rage at me after inquiries like this and tells me how beautiful I am. I am disgusted by his reactions to her miscarriage, his impatience with her grieving. I am revolted that he can say this about his wife and then tell me how attractive I was pregnant. He then often jumps to describe a current work crises. I am *just* trying to keep up.

His chaos continues to unfold as he rumples his bags of food he brings into each session: Hostess Ding Dongs, a huge bottle of Coke, and a bag of chips. I am again reminded of a teenager or child as he slurps and eats, spilling food down his shirt. He laughs at what a mess he is. I cringe at the crumbs being spilled on my couch and his sticky fingers grasping onto my delicate throw pillows. Before I know it, he is up and out the door for a break to use the bathroom. He closes the door behind him, silence takes over the chaos—finally. And I take a deep breath. I *again* try to unravel the feelings of being disrespected, angry, used, out of control, while desperately trying to understand him and what he needs. I feel like I am always just keeping up with David, one step behind the trail of destruction he leaves in his path. As these chaotic experiences continue the therapist becomes less able to use reverie and symmetrically elaborate her experience of the patient. Like her patient, the therapist becomes overwhelmed, unable to alter the concrete asymmetrical position that she is in, thinking in terms of bits and pieces.

He tells me stories of his upbringing—how he became a businessman at a very young age. Sneaking out of school to sell candy or cassette tapes–contraband—until the rabbi would find him and scold him. He loved breaking the rules—he *needed* to break the rules. Sometimes during sessions—when I feel like things are progressing nicely—he weeps and relates how saddened he is by his inability to feel love, about his divorce, and the loss of dear friends. I feel good. I feel like we are doing "good work." But then the tides shift . . . and I feel the waves begin to crash—at this time he has begun singing, performing one of his favorite hits from the early 1990s. His voice cracks, his eyes are closed—he is really feeling this. I understand right away that this is not to be interpreted. Let him be in this. I was at first delighted by this . . . how interesting it was that he would break into song to relate his experience to me! What a symbolic experience he is having! Wow, he is really "processing" his past into useful mindful working images. The first time he sang in my office it was as he talked about his conflict of being religious—how he felt so committed to Judaisim, but resented the rules and repression, he sang R.E.M.'s (Berry, Buck, Mills & Stipe, 1991) number one song "Losing My Religion." Brilliant I thought, as he sang and I tapped my foot to the music. This is just brilliant. He goes on, "That's me in the corner. There's me in the spotlight, losing my religion!" Little did I know, this was only the *beginning* of his therapeutic stage performances.

Soon my musical experiences with him started to be less than enjoyable. He began doing his best attempt at serenading me. But it felt more like he was hunting me. Usually the crooning occurs immediately after having a more intimate revealing moment with him, one in which he has felt something within our relationship, within himself. It's like he steps out of his feeling self, into a *character*—some kind of bad Don Juan impersonator. His eyes become beady, he lowers his glance a bit, takes off his glasses and begins to sing. His favorite is "Hero," by Enrique Inglesias. As he sings to me my whole body becomes tense. "I'll be your hero, baby! I can kiss away the pain. I'll stand by you forever. You can take my breath away." I hear myself begin to talk over his singing, trying desperately to climb out from under him. I feel like he is pinning me down, locking me up, making me "his." I CAN*NOT* think. I am speaking, but I am not getting through to him, but I continue. If I am silent—and I have tried this—it goes on longer and becomes even more intense, and *doesn't* feel helpful. The times I have been quiet, I feel guilty like I am letting him "do things to me." I feel like we've stepped over a line. So I revert to saying something, anything, any lame attempt at a shallow interpretation. I feel like I have to speak to just feel alive during these times with him. I am scrambling. I feel powerless. I think, how this must look from the outside? What am I doing here? The entire frame of therapy feels blown out of the water—here my patient is singing to me? And I feel trapped? How can this be? Once he stops singing, he tells me that he can rescue me at any time . . . if I have a flat tire, call him. If I need money—ever—he will lend it to me. Although he seems so sincere, I am so aggravated. Mostly, I think, because he constructs this situation where it seems I cannot respond in any way that gets us out of this moment. This is actually where he wants to be—me feeling powerless and him saving me.

He has recently told me that within his family you always knew someone would rescue you if you were in bona fide need—they'd save you. If you needed a fire put out, money, someone beat up, you got it. But you didn't "have anyone" by your side otherwise. You are either the savior or the one being saved. If only these two roles exist, wouldn't you, too, want to be the savior? My working images—the terrifying crashing wave, him the savior, me feeling caged by him—these metaphors often feel whole and have a story—a beginning, an end. However, *oftentimes*, after being with David 20 minutes into session and experiencing his firm avoidance of his internal world, I begin to not be able to access any of this thought, life, breath. Especially when he becomes flirtatious, remarks on my appearance, or answers one of my robust questions with "you know how I feel, you know what I want, I want you." I can feel my thoughts literally evaporate. This feels—

and *I feel*—anything but sexual. I have thought how I *wished* it felt sexual since it can feel such the opposite of sensual or spontaneous. My analytic well, usually so full, flowing, is *empty*. My mind feels stolen by him. There is a script he brings and it can feel so incredibly enduring. I literally feel like I am unable to reflect outside of these horribly assigned sexual roles. "This isn't like me." I mull over, I can usually imagine in such expansive ways, *I* can hold a roomful of false selves. But with David I can feel so incredibly concrete—that is, if I can think at all. This is when I know that my analytic container is broken and leaking all over.

By admitting and feeling my reactions to him more and more, I am just now beginning to grasp how I can step outside my saturated experience enough to feel it for "us," but not become overwhelmed by it. I am learning how to contain him and our experience together—his affects, his needs, my affects, my self. I am beginning to truly understand—and experience what it means to contain a patient therapeutically and not only "hold" him. I am learning to free my mind into use while he tries to control me, make me into a statue, and exhume my subjectivity. I continue to examine David's ambivalence about our relationship, his wish to keep me and others at a safe distance with his chaotic performance, while alternately acting out in intrusive and sexual ways. Since his compulsive behaviors act as stand-in for relationships for him—permeable containers that always leave him empty—I am trying to be less directive, which is just so tempting, and instead just be with him more. I am doing my best to stand alongside this process together making more use of the "analytic third" while resisting controlling the framework of the session. I am getting better at accepting what is, and not worrying so much about some professional responsibility for our sessions to fit into some preconstructed analytic model. He is one patient that I must literally "meet" again for the first time each occasion he enters my office. All of my preconceived ideas about "our work" vanish and I must literally be in the moment with him. When I am able to do this, and be more in my reverie, I feel calm—*and alive*. Enlivened by the sheer energy of this man—he is making it in the world but playing by his *own* rules this time around—even therapeutically. This week when he leaves, I will again stand to say goodbye, close the door, and turn to wipe the crumbs, the frosting, the bits of chips off my couch. I'll dump them into the trash can and feel like I am organizing the toys after my baby's gone to bed. Putting the stuff where it belongs. After all, I am here to contain him and hopefully, eventually, help him somehow clean up this mess.

LEXIE[3]

At our initial meeting, Lexie pranced into my office as if she hadn't a care in the world; she breezed in as if making an entrance for a bevy of suitors. She wore layers of satiny, shiny clothing. She was very, very thin. She smiled coyly, batted her eyes, and said "Hey," quite convincingly casual. Wearing thick eye make-up and heavily bejeweled for an early morning appointment, she explains, with an apparent air of insight and humor, her history with anorexia and bulimia and her dysfunctional family. She reports to have conquered her eating disorder by herself (no treatment needed), and that she was doing great now. She assured me her relationship with food was "much better," that she no longer restricts and would only on occasion binge and purge when overwhelmed or upset. Basically, she explained, she was seeking treatment because her girlfriend thought she needed it. The problem, in her opinion, was a long-distance relationship. It was this relationship, she purported, which was triggering this resurgence of her binging and purging behavior.

This first meeting with Lexie was my first week back from a four-month maternity leave; I was bleary-eyed from lack of sleep, and having left my first child for the first time. I had spoken with Lexie on the phone a month or so before my maternity leave. I told her that I was not taking any new patients at the current time, due to the pregnancy and subsequent time away, but that I would be happy to refer her to several other therapists. I asked her about herself to get a sense of why she was seeking treatment and for whom to refer her to. We spoke for about 10 minutes and I gave her the names of several different colleagues. She emailed me toward the end of my leave, asking if she could have an appointment with me upon my return, that she hadn't really "clicked" with the other therapists and she wanted to work with me. Flattery, it seems, will get you everywhere . . .

I had decided a year or so earlier to stop treating low weight anorexic patients in my practice. I actually was not taking any medically unstable eating disorder patients; I was feeling self-protective due to my pregnancy and some preceding medical situations and felt that the anxiety of managing the medical piece that often accompanies patients with severe eating disorders would be too great for me to bear. But Lexie was not anorexic, she purported. She loved food, and detailed her daily variety of carbohydrate-rich and calorie-dense food (not your typical anorectic fare).

I began noticing that I was acting differently with Lexie than I would with other patients. I was overlooking her obvious low body weight (she claimed "small boned" for her 5'7" 110 pound body) making this exception to my recent "no-anorexic" rule. I was losing track of time and was having trouble ending sessions. I found myself noticing her clothes, her person, much more than I do with other patients. "Nice shoes," I found myself saying week after week about her myriad footwear. Her shirts would occasionally be unbuttoned uncomfortably low. I began feeling uncomfortable and disoriented, unable to remember what I was about to say—what I wanted to say. (I also found myself feeling physically "starving" after our sessions.) It was also around this time that Lexie began to disclose aspects of her life, a reality that was terribly hard for me to swallow. I began to hear vivid details of her eating disorder.

As the months went on and the "everything is fabulous" façade began to fade, I soon learned that a typical evening for Lexie involves her anesthetizing herself in order to allow for some food, some nourishment, to enter her body. She would take whatever prescription or non-prescription drugs she could get her hands on, drink a bottle of wine, then eat all the food she had restricted throughout the day. She would then spend hours vomiting out the contents of her stomach. She will vomit, sometimes, until she sees blood. She can vomit soundlessly, she claims. She is so adept at her bulimia, the vomit cascades out at will. In actuality her eating disorder, her anorexia and bulimia, was in full force and had never abated. I had been duped.

Sometime around this time, I began to feel a visceral repulsion. I found myself feeling quite literally disgusted. I began feeling ashamed, that I was so disoriented and drained by the end of the sessions. I must be a horrible therapist, I thought. My capacity to think was limited and I was just paying attention to the surface. I felt I was just barely "holding on." Was it my disorientation with new motherhood, missing my newborn son, juggling work and primary maternal preoccupation? Had giving birth somehow diminished my capacity to think? I found myself fixating on external, disturbing minutiae. Did she touch the vomit? Did she have time to shower after? Is that vomit I now smell? I found myself so aware of her physical person, much more so than with other patients (or with myself). How can she be out in the world "functioning" after the evening she just had? Her eyes aren't even bloodshot (mine were!). I soon started realizing that Lexie was not functioning; she was merely going through the motions. The extremes of Lexie's self-annihilating behavior were shocking to me. I could not stomach it. She regularly sought out dangerous, sexual interactions and would detail them to me during our therapy sessions with little to no affect.

The previous paragraph describes the beginning of the collapse of the analyst's capacity to contain the patient's evacuated affective states. It is as if the contents of the mind and the contents of the stomach have become merged in a series of paranoid, concrete, asymmetrical moments. The analyst feels intense shame which I believe is often an indication of the collapse of the container contained aspect of therapy.

When I listened to her detailed accounts I could not stand hearing it. She purported to feel "fine" and "nothing much" about the physical violence and verbal and apparent sexual assaults she encountered.

References to her family and childhood were few and far between. Information was used like casual, humored explosives, creating a fragmented account of her past. Her mother was beautiful and her father was successful. Her mother had been to many different alcohol treatment programs. Her father was a work-obsessed alcoholic who hit her with belts. Her mother had left Lexie and her father when she was six years old to move in with her lover, a possessive and painfully insecure anorexic woman. Lexie had been raised by random babysitters.

Often I found myself looking in a hanging mirror in my office closet after she left (something I usually don't do after seeing a patient). I found myself looking white as a ghost with a look of dismay and disbelief on my face, feeling drained and overwhelmed and thinking: I look a mess!! It's all about appearances, Lexie would say. I could not contain her or myself. I could not think or organize my thoughts. I experienced the intolerable and sickening horror that she could not. She evacuates the emotional component, everything she is not experiencing on the inside, and recreates it on the outside. I question whether she has the experience of her body as a solid container, and my failure at this point to contain her.

The therapist is describing her experience of a loss of differentiation between the patient and herself in terms of time, place, and person. These dimensions of reality collapse and she becomes one with her patient's experience. Moments like this are very frightening and shameful when the therapist loses a sense of self. However, it is helpful to recognize that these experiences are often precursors to reverie and a capacity to repair the broken container.

I decided to discuss Lexie in my supervision group to help me manage my feelings and to muddle forward. I tried to speak about Lexie and articulate my transference. But I found my disgust and shame quite disorienting. I again could not think, could not articulate my feelings, what was happening in the room; I was completely shut down. I felt full of shame for having such a strong negative reaction and panic about exposing my failure as a therapist to the group. I felt responsible and worried about Lexie's health and physical safety. I worried that she could overdose or contract a disease.

I began insisting that Lexie seek out medical care and see an internist and speak with a psychiatrist. She would agree, then disappear from treatment for weeks at a time. I began to worry if she didn't come back, and then I found myself worrying, WHAT IF SHE DID? For a period of three months, Lexie came to therapy only about once or twice a month and would call and cancel on the day of the appointment to all other sessions.

The therapist is beginning to feel separate from her merged state of psychic and symbolic equivalence with her patient and is beginning to recover her ability to think and to act with a sense of concern and authority.

It is a painful, exhausting process avoiding one's own feelings. The relational and interpersonal wrenching and the physical and intrapsychic torture leave Lexie physically and emotionally bereft and depleted. She recreates her internal experience externally—the violence, the neglect, the self annihilation, and abuse. It is as if all that is inside is now on the outside. Her eating disorder symptomatology, her continual state of hunger, feeling deprived, being in this perpetual state of need, feeling starved. She deprives her need for food, for nourishment; she deprives her need for love and connection. She then gorges on what she has needed or wanted all day then violently forces, regurgitates it all back up. Similarly, the woman she loves is only occasionally in-town and Lexie's emotional needs are only sometimes satisfied.

Recently, Lexie told me that she feels like she does not exist unless she is "being seen." She feels more at ease in public places, although not engaging with people. Home feels excruciatingly lonely and empty, she said. When she is seen she feels like she exists. Her parents communicated that her internal experiences do not matter, that it is her external presence that matters. She recently had a dream: She was at her old house, where she spent some time as a child. Outside there was an imminent threat. She looks out the window and sees her mother smoking a cigarette. She goes down to the kitchen, where there is a container of explosives. She tried to push it out, but she couldn't. The closer she got to the container, the sicker she felt. She started yelling for her family to come down and help but they don't hear. Her family was not coming. Suddenly there is an explosion and everything is destroyed. She wants to go to her mom, but in a weird way, felt that her mom was responsible. The bottom floor is not destroyed, but everything is broken. Lexie becomes upset and anxious! She keeps feeling in the dream that her mom is responsible and wonders why she doesn't come.

This dream illustrates the recovery of the container contained function and the beginning of a process of symbolization. The patient is able to articulate and symbolize her experience of danger in her childhood home and as she does this she is able to experience and reflect on her feelings and the unavailability of a care taking person. Simultaneously, the analyst is also able to symbolize this dream with her concern that she is the unavailable mother, that she is failing the patient, that she can contain and experience her potential guilt. In this moment the analyst is able to become the disowned object and to participate through reverie in a symmetrical symbolic moment.

When Lexie started coming regularly to therapy again, I brought up our work together and what was going on between us, and she strongly denied that there was any "us"; we had no relationship. The following week, she sent me an angry email that said I was not helping her and wasn't that my job? I began to feel more present with Lexie. She was overwhelming me less and communicating more. I was able to get a sense of what she was feeling. Around this time she also decided to stop having anonymous, violent sex with strangers. Recently, Lexie started seeing a psychiatrist and nutritionist I recommended. She has been prescribed medication. She claims that for the first time in her life, she is not binging and purging, going on 45 days, and that she is eating four small meals a day. She claims to have gained six or seven pounds. But I'm not quite sure if I believe her.

NOTES

1. Freud without explanation switches the gender in his comment from that of the female patient to a male pronoun.
2. Reale, K., (2010). Trying to Clean Up the Mess: Chaos and Control in the Analytic Space. Paper presented at the spring meeting of Division 39, Chicago, IL.
3. Darcy, M., (2010). Spicy Inside-Out Roll: Dealing with Revulsion in the Analytic Space. Paper presented at the spring meeting of Division 39, Chicago, IL.

Chapter Eight

Learning to Ride a Bicycle

Procedural and Narrative Processes in Supervision

We all remember the moment that we learned to ride a bicycle. I remember the day I learned to ride my bicycle: we were on a path near Sheepshead Bay and my father held the bicycle as he ran alongside of me until I had the confidence to balance it by myself. Overcoming the fear of falling, trusting my father, and trusting myself was thrilling. I was completely ecstatic; I felt I was flying. Learning to ride a bicycle is often used as an illustration of the multidimensional, nonlinear, nonlinguistic aspects of procedural learning. The differences between procedural and narrative learning becomes very clear when we try to verbally instruct someone on how to ride a bicycle, dance, or flirt. The concept of procedural learning emerged in the context of neuropsychological and cognitive science and contributes an important perspective to understanding psychoanalysis and psychotherapy which involve parallel processes of narrative and procedural learning which may be located in the left and right brain systems for processing of information. The BPCSG (2007) emphasizes the importance of procedural learning in describing the intersubjective process of developing schemas of relationships that become encoded through repeated experiences (RIGS) (Stern, 1985) involving implicit relational knowing. The metaphor of learning to ride a bicycle highlights the importance of procedural learning in mastering complex relational experiences involved in both living in intersubjective, intimate relationships and in doing psychoanalysis and psychotherapy. The complex cognitive and emotional capacities that are developed through procedural learning involve more than integrating complex systems of kinesthetic and sensory feedback; they involve complex intersubjective elements such as an awareness of one's own and the other's intentionality, being willing to take a risk, possibly being hurt and alternatively hurting the other, letting go of our "observing ego," and trusting that we won't be laughed at when we make fools of our selves, as we fall down over and over again.

PROCEDURAL LEARNING IN PSYCHOTHERAPY AND SUPERVISION

Psychoanalytic supervision involves two overlapping dyads; that of the therapist and supervisor and the therapist and patient. In both dyads there is a narrative dimension involving the exchange of information and a procedural dimension in which unconscious enactments emerge and structure the intersubjective relationship developing from concrete actions to a symbolic discourse. Learning to do psychoanalysis involves both narrative and procedural learning. The narrative aspects of learning include understanding the evolution of psychoanalytic concepts, choosing among the many theoretical models of the mind which fits a particular patient therapist dyad, being able to describe the evolving transference-countertransference matrix and the relationship between early developmental experiences and the patient's personality and psychopathology. The narrative aspects of psychoanalysis are learned in classes and in reading theoretical papers and books which develop an understanding of the coordinates of the psychoanalytic relationship, the maps through which we can locate our patients and ourselves in multiple dimensions of space and time. The narrative[1] aspects of doing psychoanalysis are also learned in mentoring relationships with one's own analyst/therapist, colleagues, and supervisors and are often quite explicit. We are told what something means, how to set boundaries, assume a professional role in relation to a patient, and most importantly to verbalize our interpretations and interventions. Procedural learning is harder to describe and is learned implicitly, in one's own therapy and in the implicit relational dimension (BPCSG, 2007) of supervision. Procedural learning involves developing the capacity to respond to the complex multiple channels of information and feedback in the expanding relationship between patient and analyst and analyst and supervisor. It involves the development of trust in self and the other and the courage to take the risks, to make mistakes, and accept the possibility of hurting the patient, feeling shame and embarrassment. The "marked" responses that parents give children in which affect or content may be exaggerated is clearly part of the implicit dimension of procedural learning

Bateson et al. (1968) were among the pioneers in the development of family therapy and studied the relationship between interpersonal communication, psychopathology, and treatment interventions. They described two dimensions which are elements of all communication: an explicit dimension of content, or information that functions like the discursive or narrative aspect of communication and psychotherapy, and an implicit dimension which functions like a series of commands, similar to the procedural dimension, which they conceptualized as a set of embedded instructions on how to understand a particular message, respond to the speaker, and structure the relationship. One of the examples (Bateson et al., 1968) that illustrate how these two dimensions operate within family therapy with a family that had a schizophrenic member, a young adult who had been hospitalized, sharply illustrates the difference between information, the narrative dimension, and the implicit command function that organizes the intersubjective relationship, the procedural dimension. The patient gave his mother a Mothers Day card that said: "You have been just like a Mother to me." The family flew into a disorganized state of intense emotion, seemingly threatened by their child's communication, and trying to insist that the patient didn't understand that his mother was actually his mother and not a person who was like a mother to him. While the family focused on the error on the level of the narrative, the family's chaotic disorganization illustrated the implicit power that had been given to the patient to define or reveal the family's success and failure, perhaps further suggesting that this young person's implicit role was to reveal the family's secrets and the family pathology.

Winnicott (1971a) was an important theorist who seemed quite conversant in operating on the implicit procedural dimension of psychoanalysis and psychotherapy. Winnicott's development of the concept of transitional experience as necessary for the development of symbolization and his understanding of psychotherapy and psychoanalysis as subcategories of play are quite similar to the contemporary concept of procedural learning. Winnicott (1971a) was reluctant to present clinical examples of his own work, often stating that he strongly believed that each analyst needed to find his/her own language and own voice. Those of Winnicott's interpretations that are available always sound quite simple, direct, and have a procedural focus, while simultaneously interweaving theoretical and narrative elements.

An interesting example of Winnicott's interpretative style is presented by Guntrip (1975) in his description of his first few analytic sessions with Winnicott. He described Winnicott as reaching right into the core of his unresolved problems through what we might think of as his use of procedural interpretations. In his first session, Winnicott, (Guntrip, 1975, p. 152) perhaps feeling a silent demand from Guntrip, said: "if I don't say something, you may begin to feel I'm not here." A similar interpretation of describing his experience of being simultaneously present and absent was followed in the second session with a further attempt to develop a procedural experience in which Guntrip would feel contained and held: "You know about me, but I'm not a person to you yet. You may go away feeling alone and that I'm not real. You must have had an earlier illness before Percy was born, and felt mother left you to look after yourself. You accepted Percy as your infant self that needed looking after. When he died, you had nothing and collapsed." Although Winnicott in the second part of the interpretation presents a narrative explanation, the primary focus of the interpretation is creating a now moment in which Winnicott recognizes Guntrip's experience of not being real, not being seen, and attempts to connect, through his process of symmetrization, collapsing the difference between Guntrip's sense of nonexistence and his own experience of not yet being real describing as a presentational moment Guntrip's experience of his early life after his brother died. Winnicott collapsed the affective and literal space between them, symmetrizing and symbolizing these experiences and becoming the one who contains and is able to tolerate the sense of nonexistence (nonbeing) stating: "you may begin to feel I'm not here," "I'm not a person to you yet," "and that I'm not real." I believe that Winnicott's interpretations functioned like a good parent, holding his son on a bicycle, in order for the son to develop trust in both himself and his parent. It also seems that Winnicott was willing to take the risk of actively bringing himself into the center of the relationship, creating a now moment in which he may fall down and be rejected.

PSYCHOANALYTIC SUPERVISION

Many contemporary relational analysts have focused on the intersubjective elements in the supervisory process. Sarnat (2014) presents her supervision of a difficult analysis. In this supervision, feelings of worthlessness are described as having "paralleled up" from the analysis into the supervision relationship. The supervisor and the analyst's overlapping vulnerability to feelings of worthlessness were activated, leading to an atmosphere of dissociation and deadness in the supervision. The impasse in supervision contributed to a parallel impasse in the analysis. Sarnat consulted with her peers in order to address this impasse. Because her peers were outside of the dissociative dynamic that had settled over the supervision, they experienced warmth and empathy toward the patient, which revived the patient for Sarnat. Exploration of the "dissociative retreat" in supervision allowed Sarnat to revive compassion and connection with her supervisee. Following the consultation with her peers Sarnat resumed supervision with renewed confidence. She and the supervisee began to face the difficulties that had created the impasse in an open manner, including mutual acknowledgement of their vulnerabilities. In turn, the supervisee's confidence and compassion were revived within the analysis, allowing her to connect with the patient again. Her anxieties decreased, creating space for her to appreciate the patient's experiences and to communicate more effectively. This is an illustration of a failure in the supervisory processes, like the one discussed in chapter 6 on dissociation, where patient, analyst, and supervisor all became dissociated, felt sleepy and deeply ashamed. In her discussion of the parallel process between supervision and psychoanlaysis, Sarnat emphasizes the narrative elements of this impasse which she thinks of as a supervisory enactment, and she encourages other supervisors to be alert to the exploration of the analyst's and supervisor's contributions to transference-countertransference blockages as a means of resolving the dissociation and as an opportunity for growth for both participants.

Berman (2000) presents a similar intersubjective perspective on the supervisory process and believes that the analyst's personal dynamics are an unavoidable topic for exploration in supervision. He believes that the supervisory relationship also develops independent transference-countertransference structures which need to be explored, "acknowledged and allowed as potential legitimate contents in the supervisory discourse." If there is avoidance of these dynamics then supervision may become stilted or oppressive. The complex transference countertransference enactments that occur in supervision have been thought of as an unconscious recreation of the transference countertransference dynamic that originated between the patient and therapist. These therapeutic enactments have been described as "parallel processes" (Bass, 2004b) intersubjective experiences that become a source of information about the enacted transference countertransference relationship. Ogden (2005, p. 1268) critiques this concept of parallel process, suggesting that it is too passive, emphasizing the narrative aspect of enactments over the experiential dimension of procedural learning. He describes the overlapping dyads of the analyst and patient and the analyst and supervisor as "liv(e)ing in muscular tension with one another, (and are) all the time re-contextualizing and altering one another." Ogden believes that "the analytic relationship and the supervisory relationship constitute two facets of a single set of conscious and unconscious internal and external object relationships involving supervisor, supervisee and patient." Ogden (2005) describes the spontaneity of the supervisory relationship as an emergent experience, like the analytic third (ref), a dream, or the construction of therapeutic play space like Winnicott's (1971a) concept of transitional experience.

Ogden (2005) raises the question: "Who is the patient whose analysis is the subject of the supervision?" He suggests that the "analyst does not bring the (actual) analysand to the supervisory session; rather (with the help of the supervisor), the analyst 'dreams up' the patient in the supervisory setting. In other words, the patient who is brought to life in supervision is not the living, breathing person who lies on the analyst's couch. Rather, the patient who is presented in the supervisory session is a fiction created in the medium of words, voice, physical movements (e.g. the supervisee's hand gestures), irony, wit, (and) unconscious communications such as projective identifications . . . " It is important to acknowledge that patient being discussed in supervision is not the same person who the analyst sees, but a creation of supervisor and analyst, a new subject who "is dreamed up" in the symbolic, transitional play space of the supervisory relationship.

CREATION OF A TRANSITIONAL SPACE

It is important to recognize the need to create a safe space in which both supervisor and supervisee can freely talk about the inherently frightening, dangerous, evaluative elements of supervision, as well as the nightmare-like feelings of isolation, the dark anxieties and responsibilities inherent in doing psychoanalytic psychotherapy. Winnicott (1971a) describes psychotherapy and psychoanalysis as subcategories of the universal experience of play, asserting that the essential characteristic of play is an experience of "purposelessness," which he implicitly contrasts with the purposefulness and goal directness of work. From Winnicott's perspective narrative, purposeful, instructional approaches to supervision where the supervisor attempts to direct or "control" the treatment presented by the analysand in supervision are more like work and procedural approaches to supervision are more like play.

Meltzer (Oelsner, R. & Oelsner, M., 2005, p. 457) a Kleinian analyst, suggests that it is the supervisor's task to make the supervisee feel safe enough to freely talk about their thoughts and experiences. Meltzer, like many of us, uses humor as a way of creating this safe, transitional space in which procedural learning may occur. In talking about his work with supervisees, Meltzer states that "If I can help him, first of all, to present that patient vividly, so that I can make contact with the patient, then I feel that we have a real supervision. I feel that I am in contact both with the patient and with the analyst, and can introduce them to one another, and that is very enjoyable. I always feel about psychoanalysis that if it isn't fun it's probably not very good. I like to enjoy myself. So the use of humor and wit seem to me to be very important, not only in supervision, but in analysis. I like every session to end with a smile." Meltzer's emphasis on humor and enjoyment in both analysis and supervision is a breath of fresh air that underscores the transitional and playful aspects of supervision, psychoanalysis, and other intersubjective experiences that involve procedural learning.

In structuring the supervisory relationship as a procedural experience, the supervisor needs to disavow the asymmetrical position of authority inherent in the hierarchical structure of education and psychoanalysis, creating a symmetrical, emotionally vulnerable space for transitional experiences and play. Many authors have critiqued assumptions of power in the psychoanalytic relationship including Mitchell (1998), suggesting that analytic authority is based on our ability to engage in relationships which enrich and expand the experience of living rather than a superior position of knowing and speaking the truth. Similarly, Lacan (1981) criticizes the analyst's assumption of authority, noting that this experience of authority reflects an organization of experience within the imaginary sphere as the supervisor or analyst presenting him/her self as "the one who is supposed to know" while actually being in the dark. Bion (1965) espouses symmetrical (Newirth, 2003), egalitarian, values encouraging both analysts and supervisors to maintain a "negative capability," not knowing, and maintaining radical doubt. Developing an egalitarian, symmetrical relationship, and minimizing authority, is an important goal in supervision, an achievement, as the relationship progresses, involving more and more procedural elements, as both participants become free to comment on each other's behavior.

I asked past and current supervisees to write about their experiences in order to better understand what went on from the perspective, the vertice, of the supervisee. One supervisee, commenting on the development of trust in our relationship, said: "It's hard to speak to the times when I felt that I couldn't trust you, but I remember vividly being able to say to you during our hour together, time and time again, that I didn't trust you! And that alone, I think, made it a safer place to do the work. I named it, which gave me a sense of control, however false, over the uncontrollable situation. Being able to challenge your authority without (serious) repercussions, or inflicting damage (in a Winnicottian sense?)—on you—without lasting effects was important to developing my own sense of significance and a voice that I could carry with me into the therapy rooms."

Another supervisee, a man, began our work with a strong desire to feel like a successful analyst; that generated a great deal of evaluative, persecutory anxiety in our relationship. He presented his work with a difficult woman with whom he was both quite attached and often angry. She undermined his confidence, his idealized image of himself, presenting herself as desperate, often challenging him with unsolvable problems. We had been working together for a while when he discussed a session that had made him very anxious because this woman was threatening suicide which included her having somewhat realistic plans. He was quite anxious in supervision and I must have been listening in a fairly unresponsive way. He remembers telling me "that there was something weird about how detached you seemed about this patient threatening suicide, being difficult, etc." This is one of those difficult moments when a supervisee is feeling on the verge of falling apart (falling down) and is calling out for help to an apparently unresponsive supervisor. As with learning to ride a bicycle, it is up to the supervisor to be able to maintain a calm and confident belief in the supervisee's ability to move forward whether he falls down or not. My response, which feels embarrassing, I hope that you are able to read it as spoken in an ironic voice, what Meltzer (Oelsner, R. & Oelsner, M., 2005) referred to as the music which accompanies the words, was: "Look, I just came back from a nice lunch, I'm sitting here comfortably in my office, feeling relaxed, and you have this person who is threatening suicide, making you miserable." Sometimes I am surprised at the things I say; I sound dismissive and hostile, sometimes I think I sound like a real jerk. However, my supervisee heard something different in my words, he heard a more playful comment that reframed the situation from the immediacy of the paranoid anxiety of feeling responsible for a suicidal patient, to an experience in which we could have some room to think and hopefully enjoy our moment together. In reflecting on this moment, he said: "Something about that struck me—I think it shifted my thinking of you in the moment—from being persecutory, superior and detached, to being calm and outside of the fray enough to be reassuring/helpful."

This supervisee described another time when he was really worried about his patient: "Something had happened, I think she had done badly on something she needed to do to get into graduate school, and she was very unsteady. She asked me to call her, and when I did she was basically silent, uncommunicative on the phone. This call left me feeling very irritated and worried. When I told you about it, you said: "that you feel miserable about it which means that it was a successful phone call. That was really helpful, and helped me understand something about projective identification." Again, hearing my words feels embarrassing and raises my paranoid anxiety about being exposed, judged, and humiliated. Although intellectually I know it is inevitable to feel vulnerable when describing and organizing supervision as a form of play, a transitional experience, a process of dreaming the patient into existence, a form of procedural learning, I worry about being judged!

DEVELOPMENT OF TRUST

Supervision evolves from states of frozenness, anxiety, and panic, to opportunities for mutual play and the development of a generative perspective, creating meaning, dreaming the unconscious experiences of patient and therapist and therapist and supervisor into existence, through the creation of symbols and metaphors. This process requires that a relationship of trust becomes firmly established. Meltzer (Oelsner, R. & Oelsner, M., 2005) describes the process of developing trust in the following way: "Well, what you hope (he) the supervisee brings in an honest description of the experience with a particular patient. And the emphasis is on the honest because, until an analyst knows his supervisor well enough to begin to enjoy the supervision, it's very difficult for him to be honest. The building up of this kind of trust between supervisor and analyst is essential, because, until it reaches a level where it is a pleasure to come to supervision, you won't get honest material; and, of course, to work with material that is not honest is like walking in the marsh."

However, not all supervisory relationships feel like an honest, playful, procedural experience, something we look forward to. Many supervisory relationships do not develop safety and trust, procedural learning fails; supervisor and supervisee get stuck, going through the motions and counting the hours until it finally ends. I have had several experiences in supervision in which trust and safety did not develop; I will describe one. I was working with an extremely perceptive, paranoid woman who dreamt that I was speaking with an older man about our psychoanalytic work and that he was being very critical of me. I imagined my patient was dreaming about my current supervisor, a critical and frightening person to me. I believe that this patient unconsciously experienced my dread of this supervisor and was trying to help me (Searles, 1979) deal with him in a more productive way, since she thought that our analytic work was going quite well. However, rather than confronting my fears and my supervisor, I chose a cowardly approach and began presenting a different patient in supervision. This was a missed opportunity, I did not trust myself, the supervisor, or the analytic process. Farber (1999) describes a similar experience of failure in his work in supervision with Freda Fromm-Reichmann, in a paper titled "Lying on the Couch." She insists that he is feeling angry toward her and the patient and she does not believe him when he insists that he is not feeling angry. Farber eventually relents and gives the supervisor what she wants, and tells her that he is angry with her, while knowing that this is a fiction, a lie, reflecting a failure in the development of trust in the supervision. In both of these examples the supervisor was unable to switch from a narrative approach to a procedural approach in which the anxieties in the supervision relationship could become addressed in a nonjudgmental way. Often these supervisory enactments leave both participants feeling trapped and imprisoned. I believe that it is ultimately up to the supervisor to break this cycle, sometimes, saying their thoughts that may confirm the supervisee's worst fantasies. Bion (1965) describes moments like this as his feeling/being free to think his own thoughts. His demonstration of this freedom can function as a model for procedural rather than narrative learning.

The development of trust, for both participants, involves taking risks, often feeling guilty because the lines between analysis and supervision become blurred when focusing on the supervisee's and supervisor's countertransference and character. Berman (2000), a relational analyst, encourages an open and mutual exploration of countertransference and believes that this leads the analyst and supervisor to experience inner freedom, which in turn generates a transitional space that is conducive to creativity and generating new meanings that could not be achieved with a one person narrative approach. Ferro (2006, p. 991), a contemporary Kleinian analyst, presents a slightly different perspective, approaching the supervisory situation as a "psychoanalytic game," a concept developed by Bion, in which both participants attempt to affectively and symmetrically elaborate their experience within the supervisory relationship, encouraging the free play of dream thoughts, reverie, and symbolization. Thinking of the supervisory experience as a "psychoanalytic game" reframes the traditional concern about not maintaining a separation between psychoanalysis and supervision into a singular pursuit, developing and maintaining the analyst's and supervisor's minds, their capacity for reverie and symbolization. Ferro (2006) believes that Bion's work shifted our attention from the contents of thought, the narrative dimension, to the procedural dimension, the capacity to create meaning, to symbolize, and dream. Ferro (2006, p. 990) states: "The focus is no longer on a psychoanalysis that aims to remove the veil of repression or to integrate splittings, but on a psychoanalysis interested in the development of the tools that allow the development and creation of thought, that is the mental apparatus for dreaming, feeling and thinking."

This question of differences between analysis and supervision is very important and is often reflected in the question of what is appropriate content for supervision. Berman (2000) believes that supervision and analysis overlap and suggests that we should explore their interaction. He believes that personal topics are suitable for discussion in supervision and is against telling supervisees to "bring it to your analyst" when countertransference is an issue. However, he describes supervision as more selective and goal-oriented than analysis, with the topics explored because of their effect on the analyst's work and the supervision. As a supervisor, I like to feel that I am closely listening and watching the patient's and analyst's ongoing interaction which becomes the primary focus of supervision. However, I also believe that whatever the supervisee brings in will have potential relevance for the work, assuming that the content in some way is reflecting the developing unconscious dream thoughts of patient and analyst. This mixed attitude reflects the ideas of maintaining negative capability; always being uncertain about what is relevant, what is important as we engage in a process of jointly creating meaning. For example, a supervisee who I worked with in a small supervision group described her experience of the interweaving of different levels of experience in supervision stated: I think how you/we integrate personal thoughts about our life and history into the group has REALLY helped in our building and developing trust. I remember that time that I was selling my first home and I came right to group after the closing. I was fighting back tears and didn't want to take time to talk about it and you said, jokingly and warmly: "Ya know, talking about things can help . . ."

Another supervisee describes her experience developing trust in our supervision and the parallel development of her capacity to trust her own reverie in the analytic setting. I hope that her description of her experience presents an illustration of the procedural process of learning to do psychoanalysis through her/our engaging in a "psychoanalytic game," thinking together in a transitional space where the analyst, supervisor, and patient hopefully come alive.

She began by reflecting on her previous experience: from where I come from—a more conservative analytic approach which was very data/content focused—getting to the place where I could use my mind and share my mind with a supervisor was at first beyond even my aspirational awareness. Your asking me, in the quiet between moments, "what are you thinking right there?" helped me step into the now, and away from my strained efforts to remember exact content. This has been enormous for me, enabling me to approach our scheduled hour from a much more relaxed standpoint—which from my more harsh past viewpoint, I would have framed as "unprepared." Now, with even a few minutes of reflection before the hour I am bringing in what's going on with my patient, what's going on with me, my analysis, my relationship with you, and playing in that space, sharing it with you. We don't have to have the answers—whatever that means anyway. Your willingness to tell me what you're thinking, what comes to mind has shown me that we are mirroring the analytic hour and dyadic life in general. "Whose thought is it anyway?" As a result of our co-constructing shared time and space, I feel myself more comfortably doing this in my therapeutic hours.

Around Christmas I was having a very rough time. End of the year, holidays, my oldest daughter leaving for college, my dog having an emergency hospitalization, a trip canceled to an old friend's wedding. Circumstances required that I meet with you by phone one morning from home. My cleaning lady was there which required me to be in my bedroom for our call. I was sitting on my bed while we talked. In the moment we began, you allowed me to know that a dear friend of yours had died suddenly and you were feeling a significant loss. In those moments I felt an unspoken, shared quiet between us that touched me deeply. Although we continued on to talk about my patient, I carried your willingness to let me know something about where you were beyond the hour and I reached out to you briefly in an email later to say thank you. Your response and this exchange between us was moving and gave me hope about the potential for deep, meaningful, and realness in the consultation process. I felt that this experience illustrated and encouraged me to have hope, a two way direction of hope.

I approached another supervisory hour reflecting on recent sessions with my patient T without specific notes or awareness of specific content. A moment's reflection reminded me of T's cleaning out the basement and finding a portrait of his grandfather in a closet. Wondering what to do with it. Should he take it to the curb? He'd taken a photo of it and showed it to me. It looked like an ancient corporate oil painting. As I told you about it and wondered why I was telling you about it I thought about me and my relationship to T and other men in my life, including you. I thought of another patient J who is 85, like my father, and thought of my valuing my work with him—

that he will let me know him and is knowable as my father is/was not. I saw these three portraits on the wall looking down at me and loved T's image of taking it to the curb. Oh to be rid of that experience of being looked down upon. Although I cannot locate a specific thing you said or did in this hour, I look on this hour as an achievement of our work together. Our egalitarian, shared experience, mutually valued I believe. Gives me hope and I told you so.

These comments, like those of the many supervisees who shared their experiences with me are quite humbling and help me maintain trust and understand supervision as a procedural process, like learning to ride a bicycle. One of my favorite quotes from Harold Searles (1979, p. 55) about his experience doing supervision, emphasizes both the intersubjective and procedural aspects of the supervisory process. I would like to end this chapter with this quote: "I sometimes find that I try to get the supervisee to live up to my own ego-ideal aspiration, in the hope that if I can help one after another supervisee to practice what I preach, then these supervisees will be tangible persons with whom I can identify, so that hopefully, I may someday have the courage and the skill, myself, to do with patients what (so I tell them from my vast experience) they 'obviously' should set about doing. My point is that sometimes all this works successfully for both the supervisee and me as well as for the patient, and sometimes it does not; there is a continuum between clearly pathological and healthy processes here." Searles's quote is written in the language of mutual identification and growth, what I have been referring to as an evolving symmetrical symbolic relationship that develops within the relationship when there is an emphasis on procedural learning in supervision.

NOTE

1. See Schafer (1976) and Spence (1982) for discussions of the narrative dimension of psychoanalysis and psychotherapy.

Chapter Nine

Transformational Processes

Self-Reflective Thought, Metaphor, and Symbol

In beginning this final chapter I want to return to the first metaphor that I used in the introduction: nautical charts, maps that are metaphors for the theories through which we are able to locate ourselves and our patients as we traverse the dark and sometimes stormy seas of psychoanalysis and psychotherapy. Writing a book, like psychoanalysis and psychotherapy, is a journey, and as with all journeys there is an endpoint, a destination, or a series of possible destinations that provide moments when we look back and review our progress. I would like to briefly look back at our journey. An overarching theme and purpose of this book has been to describe a paradigm shift in the human sciences. This shift has taken place across multiple disciplines which have discarded the earlier view of the mind as a hierarchical system focused on structures of control and the discovery of objective facts, to the present focus on process, how we make meaning from sensory, emotional, kinesthetic, and perceptual bits of information. In following the implicit and explicit concepts developed in these multiple areas of psychology, neuroscience, and psychoanalysis, a contemporary model of the mind is emerging which functions as a transformational system. The central question that these different transformational models of the mind attempt to answer is: "How do internal and external experiences, data, social experiences, become meaningful thoughts and symbols rather than simple stimuli, signs, which demand an immediate response from the individual?" These transformational models are focused on how we learn to think, and on the development of structures that allow us to think thoughts. These transformational approaches recognize that under different conditions we are unable to think and respond or react to the immediate situation including: freezing in response to traumatic overstimulation, experiencing with absolute certainty that the other person is a persecutory object, being stuck in the concreteness of the paranoid schizoid position, or in the mode of psychic equivalence, reacting impulsively in order to discharge a particular affect.

For many theorists, the central question is, "What are the developmental and neuropsychological structures that allow for the transformation of simple, immediate sensory and affective experience into meaningful information?" "How do we think symbolically and generate meaningful narratives and procedural schemas that organize our behavior in the world of things and in the world of intimate relationships?" Fonagy's and Target's (1969, 2007) synthesis of developmental psychology focuses on the concept of mentalization, the capacity to be aware of thoughts in one's own and others' minds which are different and different from external events. The concept of mentalization overlaps a great deal with the Kleinian concept of symbolization, while also highlighting another dimension, that of reflective thought. The capacity for reflective thought is related to the Kleinian concept of "whole objects" within the depressive position; however, it adds an important intersubjective nuance, focusing on the central importance of reflecting on content of minds, both our own and that of the other people in our intersubjective environment.

The intersubjective development of mind has been central to Bion's conceptualization of the container contained as both an intrasubjective and an intersubjective description of the development of an apparatus for thinking, and the capacity to engage in symbolic thought. The BPCSG (2007) adds a nuance to the concepts of mentalization and symbolic thought, which is that we are not only interested in our own and other people's minds, but are particularly interested in, and perceive, intentionality. The concept of intentionality is extremely important because it provides a focus on the purposefulness of behavior; we are interested in where we may be going and what otsher want from us. Kohut (1984) introduced a parallel concept in describing interpretations as having three parts: a trailing edge describing the patient's history, a contemporary description of the current transference countertransference dynamics, and a leading edge, what the patient is hoping to achieve, that behavior has both hope and intentionality. Kohut's concept of a leading edge, like the concept of intentionality, argues for the purposefulness, future orientation, and hopefulness of human relations, which contrasts with a traditional positivist perspective, which focuses on the determining effects of the past.

Although we have been referring to the development of the capacity and the structures for thinking, our focus has been largely on the clinical, intersubjective aspects of thinking as it occurs in personal, affective, and intimate relationships. Cognitive psychology considers many areas of thinking in addition to those that structure intersubjective relationships including the ability to learn mathematics, reading, science, etc. However, our interest has largely been in how structures develop which create the capacity to think within the intersubjective affective realm. Transformational models separate learning about the impersonal world of information from that of the personal world of intimate relationships. For example, Schore (2011) describes differential functions of the right and left hemispheres, while others, including most psychoanalytic theories, require that we understand that their focus is only on intersubjective, emotional, and intimate relationships. Cognitive and developmental psychologists have differentiated two parallel realms of experience describing those involved in thinking about the external world as explicit/declarative, or semantic memory, as contrasted with structures that focus on intersubjective, affective, and intimate relationships which are described as implicit/procedural and autobiographical memory. Langer (1942), a philosopher and linguist, also described two systems of generating, organizing, and communicating thought, which she described as discursive symbols, which translate and contextualize meanings into historical, explanatory, or scientific systems and presentational symbols, which like forms of art induce us to identify with and experience the subjective, emotional experience of that which has been represented. I often think of these different organizations of thought as reflecting the difference between a history of war as contrasted with Picasso's powerful painting of Guernica in which we can practically hear the cries of suffering emanating from the civilians and animals during the bombing of the city of Guernica. Although Langer developed these ideas a while ago, they are similar to current concepts of declarative and narrative learning as compared to procedural learning. Lastly, Martin Buber (1970), a philosopher, separated these two parallel realms of experience, that of the impersonal, objective world of external things, history, and law and the personal or subjective world of intimate relationships, which he described as "I - It" and "I - Thou" relationships—different realms of human experience which require different forms of thinking and communication.

Matte-Blanco (1988) reframed Freud's concept of conscious and unconscious structures into functional organizations of thought that process experience and information using different forms of logic, rules of combination, for thinking about the internal world of relationships and the external world of things, science, social roles, and the law. He suggested that these two realms of experience are organized by different systems of logic, of transformation; conscious and external experience utilizes Aristotelian or asymmetrical logic in which the dimensions of person, place, time, and causality are differentiated, while intimate and emotional experience use symmetrical logic, through which we collapse differences, creating images, dream-like experiences which can be intensely saturated emotional experiences, poetic metaphors in which multiple meanings are packed into a single image or word. The Matrix of Mental Experience describes these two realms of experience as organized using different forms of logic: asymmetrical and symmetrical logic in which more mature forms of thought in the objective, external world is abstract thought, and in the subjective, internal world of intimate relationships is symbolic thought. Symbolic thought functions in the intersubjective realm consciously and unconsciously organizing emotional and intimate relationships, while abstract thought functions in the objective realm of things, science, social roles, and the law, creating principles and laws.

There is a great deal of overlap between Matte-Blanco's bi-logical theory and psychoanalytic, developmental, cognitive, and neuropsychological theorists: implicit/procedural and autobiographical memories seem to operate through symmetrical logic, while explicit/declarative and semantic memory operate through asymmetrical logic. Similarly, concepts of the container contained and reverie operate through symmetrical logic. In chapters 6 and 7 we discussed the breakdown of the container contained function in psychoanalysis and psychotherapy. When working with extremely concrete paranoid-schizoid individuals (as well as many others) there is a breakdown of the container contained function resulting in the therapist feeling and believing that he or she is the singular bad object, is unable to think, often feeling dead or dissociated, and flooded with shame. The breakdown of the container contained function is an example of extremely paranoid, concrete symmetrical experience, which results in the therapist or supervisor becoming unable to think symbolically or mentalize, often desperately attempting to regain the capacity for reverie which is a depressive or more mature symmetrical function.

In discussing the normative aspects of the collapse of the capacity for symbolic thought and mentalization in therapy and supervison, the collapse of the container contained relationship, Fonagy (2008) points out the intense affects whether of love or hate, which makes it impossible to mentalize (think in a symbolic mode) and brings us back to a state of psychic equivalence. He states:

> Neuroimaging studies have demonstrated that the activation of the attachment system (whether stimulated by maternal feelings or by romantic love) inhibits the capacity to think dispassionately about mental states (Bartels and Zeki 2000, 2004) and pushes the individual toward a mode of subjectivity that is prementalistic, concrete, teleological, or somewhat dissociated (pretend). Perhaps even more relevant is the incompatibility of intense emotional arousal and mentalizing. Emotional involvement reduces our capacity for abstract thought, as well as for self-regulation (Arnsten 1998). When we are in love we are poor at making judgments of social trustworthiness; when we are angry we are in no state to figure out what our object might be thinking or feeling. But working with—or, better, in—the transference inevitably activates attachment feelings and greater spontaneity, and this personal involvement cannot but increase countertransferential reaction. (p. 32)

This inevitable process of breakdown of the capacity to think, of rupture and repair, is an aspect of all therapies which involve an intersubjective relationship between patient and therapist. The therapist's task is to trust that he/she can slowly regain the capacity to think, a process involving procedural learning in which reverie slowly develops in which there is a symmetrical elaboration of the collapsed psychic field of the transference countertransference. The capacity to think and speak symbolically slowly returns often generating humorous, cultural, or poetic images through which the therapist develops an ability to present his/her experience as a metaphor facilitating a transformation of the patient's and therapist's experiences as well as a progressive development of each participants ability to symbolize or mentalize their experience.

METAPHOR AND THE TRANSFORMATIONAL PROCESS

Many theorists have focused on the concept of metaphor in this expanding transformational model of the mind. Metaphor has the psychological qualities of symmetrical, symbolic organizations of experience like dream thoughts and presentational symbols. Metaphor has been a central concept among psychoanalysis (Arango, 2014) for many decades. Metaphors have been used to connect theory and technique, as in Theodore Reik's (1948) idea of "listening with the third ear" which expresses something more than Freud's pragmatic concept of "free floating attention" and Civitarese's and Ferro's (2013) concept of the analytic relationship as a field, like an electromagnetic field in which there are continuous effects of the different psychological particles. Clinicians have traditionally used metaphors as an interpretive device in clinical practice,[1] and more recently theorists have begun to think of metaphor as more than a linguistic trope, as an element of mental structure which creates meaning in the intersubjective realm of emotional and intimate relationships. Before discussing contemporary concepts of metaphor it is important to recognize Lacan's (Dor, 1998) contribution to our understanding of metaphor and language in psychoanalysis.

Unlike most early European and American psychoanalysts who conceptualized human experience from a biological and evolutionary perspective, Lacan and analysts associated with the Frankfurt school (Newirth 2016), thought of psychoanalysis as embedded within social science, anthropology, economic theory, and linguistics. Lacan (1996) was particularly interested in linguistics and presented language as both the representative of and organizer of cultural experience. He believed that the inevitable coming of language disrupts the child's purely affective and immediate relationship with the parent and the world, initiating an awareness that there are rules and consequences that each person must learn and follow. This "wall of language"

(Dor, 1998) separates the child's intense desires from the culture's requirement that the child follow rules which simultaneously splits the mind into two parallel structures, an unconscious center of desire and subjectivity and a conscious center of who we are supposed to be, the self as an ego-ideal, describing the duality of who we should be as opposed to who we discover we are. Lacan believed that these now split off, or repressed desires, can only be represented linguistically through structures of metaphor and metonymy, which, like Matte-Blanco, he derived from Freud's concept of dreams. Both Lacan and Matte-Blanco thought that dream-work, processes of condensation and displacement, metaphoric and metonymic structures, represent the structure of unconscious thought. Lacan (1996) playfully illustrates his idea of metaphor as expressing unconscious and unspoken patterns and beliefs, citing Freud's famous comment on arriving in America for the Clark University lectures: "I am bringing the plague to America!" Freud's use of the metaphor of "the plague" represented his belief that the culture of America would find the psychoanalytic emphasis on self-reflective thought, destructiveness, and sexuality, the heart of psychoanalysis, anathema. I believe that Freud's use of the metaphor of the plague also represented his wish to infect us with the dis-ease that he suffered from.

Fonagy and Target (2007) discuss the contemporary development of concepts of metaphor as an aspect of our human potential for making meaning, differentiating current concepts of embodied cognition from earlier concepts which treated the mind as separated from bodily experience.[2] Particularly important in his assessment of these developments is the work of several contemporary linguists, Lakoff and Johnson (1999), and a French linguist, Fonagy (as cited in Fonagy, 2008). These contemporary linguists believe that metaphors are not simple linguistic constructions but emerge from and express bodily experiences, as when we feel the actual pain of a broken heart or feel uplifted by a lover's smile. Embodied metaphors develop in intersubjective relationships, often beginning as gestures, enactments which express moments of intersubjective conjunction and disjunction. Although Fonagy does not point this out, we may understand these metaphors developing as concrete gestures, signs, which are both empathic and communicative, perhaps developing through the mirror neuron system (Ginot, 2009; Wolf, Gales, Shane, and Shane, 2001) and slowly become patterned as RIGS (Stern, 1985) and then symbolic, metaphorical statements. Schore's (2011) suggestion of direct affective communication between right brain and right brain of individuals in an intimate relationship, and the operation of mirror neurons as the neurological substrate for emphatic and intimate relatedness, reflect presentational and procedural aspects of learning which develop in the intimate relationship between parent and child and patient and therapist.

The theory of embodied cognition suggests that metaphors and gestures develop simultaneously as representations, body experience, gestures, actions, and metaphoric enactments, which bring a continuous sense of affective bodily experience into intersubjective relationships. Fonagy and Target (2007) states that:

> all mental acts are metaphorical and through metaphor have physical as well as abstract (symbolic) meanings. The action of the thought carries metaphoric unconscious meaning. When we "grasp an idea" we may experience a feeling of well-being or "goodness" because unconsciously we reunite with the primary object. When we "grope for a meaning" at the level of gesture we find empty space where a warm body should be, and the affect state generated is one of vacuum or emptiness. When we "seize on an idea" we in a real sense jump on top of it and thus feel excited and triumphant, like a toddler claiming omnipotent control. (p. 438)

Fonagy links the development of the capacity to use metaphors and metaphoric enactments with the dynamics of attachment relationships suggesting that patients who have had difficulty in early attachment relationships will also have difficulty in developing the capacity for verbal and enacted processes of metaphoric expression. The concept of metaphoric enactments expands our discussion of the concept of procedural learning and presentational symbols in the clinical situation and the development of the capacity to transform experience from concrete signs to symbolic meaning.

Contemporary Kleinian (Civitarese & Ferro, 2013; Ferro, 2009; Ogden, 2007, 2010) analysts have begun to approach their clinical work as a process of developing metaphors in their relationship with patients. This focus on metaphors is a clinical or pragmatic development of the theoretical, abstract concepts of symbolization, alpha function and the container contained model of the analytic relationship. Ferro's description of the importance of metaphors in the analytic dialogue echoes Fonagy's comments about embodied metaphors. He states:

> They are sensible ideas—that is to say, they combine emotion and thought. They therefore restore a bodily element to the mind; they reunite psyche and soma; they reforge the "psychosomatic collusion" (Winnicott, 1974, p. 104) that is the foundation of subjectivity; they are dreams that create reality and give it a personal meaning. (p. 206)

Ogden (2010) also emphasizes the process of metaphorization as an outcome of the container contained process, including the sequence of collapse, reverie, and symbolization. It is important in understanding this clinical process to recognize that the analytic dialogue emphasizes the development of metaphors and embodied metaphorical experiences which allow for the transformation of concrete signs in the development of subjective meaning, symbols. Ogden (2010) differentiates three forms of thinking: magical thinking, dream thinking and transformational thinking. Magical thinking reflects thinking within the paranoid-schizoid position where what is real is what is in my mind, a version of symbolic or psychic equivalence. In this state denial would involve the individual not wanting to know something and erasing it from consciousness. Dream thinking involves our capacity to create meaning using reverie, symmetrical symbolic thinking, metaphoric enactments, and presentational symbols. Transformational thinking is a rare event in which a metaphor or metaphoric enactment alters the fundamental organization of meaning for an individual, as when one shifts from a habitual understanding of self and other, of relational structures, to a new more fluid understanding in which old categories become replaced by new perceptions and symbolic expressions. Ogden (2010) uses the example of Christ's switching from the rule of law to a sense of personal relatedness and responsibility, when he said, to a crowd that would stone a woman for having committed adultry, "he that has not sinned may cast the first stone." This statement moved the listeners to symmetrically identify with the woman and not use the asymmetrical thoughts of separateness and judge her.

CLINICAL ILLUSTRATIONS: METAPHOR AND THE POETIC FUNCTION

In a startling moment Winnicott (1971a) expanded his theory of creating meaning and symbolization, from the intersubjective experiences of transitional experiences and play, to suggesting a universal capacity to create meaning through the development of metaphors which he described as the poetic function. He suggested that there is an original poet in each of us: in our unconscious we are all poets. Winnicott quotes Milner who describes:

> Moments when the original poet in each of us created the outside world for us, by finding the familiar in the unfamiliar, (which) are perhaps forgotten by most people; or else they are guarded in some secret place of memory because they were too much like visitations of the gods to be mixed with everyday thinking (Milner, 1993, p. 39).

In highlighting the poetic function, Winnicott emphasized an important distinction between the asymmetrical language of the world of objects, external reality, history, and science, and the symmetrical language of subjectivity, potential space, dreams, poetry, art, literature, and intimate relationships. He emphasizes the complex processes of creating meaning that involve more than simple representational activity, linking words to events. Poetic language, metaphors, like dreams, involve deeply human, existential themes, the incorporation of sensory experiences, the use of musical elements including rhyme, rhythm, repetition, beat, and figurative language such as simile, metaphor, imagery, personifications, hyperbole, alliteration, repetition, and onomatopoeia (the use of words that imitate sounds).

As we previously suggested, Winnicott (1971a) was reluctant to provide examples of his work with patients, preferring that we each find our own voice. However, his clinical illustrations often reflect a poetic use of language which echoes a children's book, such as Doctor Seuss, in which he emphasizes rhythms, repetitions, and absurd contrasts. In speaking with a poetic rather than an objective voice, analysts may experience anxiety, as we leave a professional, asymmetrical, discursive language and expose our subjective, unconscious fantasies, subjective dream-like metaphors that expose the haunting uncertainty that we often have no idea of what we are actually doing as therapists and occasionally suspecting that we may actually be mad. The ability to tolerate the uncertainty of madness is a critical element in the use of the poetic voice and symmetrical strategies in psychoanalysis; it is imperative to overcome the many intrapsychic and intersubjective suspicions of madness to free the inherent poet from the rational, "professional" critics who stand behind us like a series of institutional policemen.

Winnicott (1971a) specifically illustrates this double experience, linking the poetic voice with madness, in a case in which he tells a patient that he knows there is a man on his couch, but hears a girl talking about penis envy. A different analyst interpreting this patient's experience would have possibly focused on castration anxiety and the oedipal narrative. I would like to present Winnicott's interpretation, which incorporates symmetrical and procedural elements of rhythm, repetition, and the paradox of our bi-sexual identities that are presented as a multidimensional complex interpretation that can be read as a poem or a page out of a children's book. I have transposed Winnicott's (1971a) words into the written form of a poem and suggest that the reader read this interpretation aloud.

> I am listening to a girl.
> I know perfectly well that you are a man
> but I am listening to a girl,
> and I am talking to a girl
> I am telling this girl
> You are talking about penis envy. (p. 98)

Upon hearing this interpretation the patient immediately acknowledges his awareness of his identification as a girl, and states that if he told anyone about this girl he would be considered mad. Winnicott comments that he was surprised by his next statement, in which he differentiated the objective language of history and the social roles of analyst and patient, from the subjective, ambiguous language of poetry. With uncharacteristic force, Winnicott rejects the patient's attempt to convert this poetic, metaphoric enactment into an asymmetrical discursive, historical interpretive process, and insists that it was he (Winnicott) who heard the girl speaking, so that it is he who must be mad. In this critical moment Winnicott demonstrates the importance of inhabiting the metaphoric enactment of the transference countertransference relationship and presents an important symmetrical symbolic interpretation.

THEORY AND THE POETIC FUNCTION

This clinical vignette highlights two important issues: the mode or language of interpretation and the goal of interpretation which more broadly reflects the goal of psychoanalysis. Mitchell (1998), writing from a relational perspective, redefined the goals of psychoanalysis and interpretation from revealing hidden truths or resolving historical conflicts to expanding and enriching patients' experiences of life. Ferro (2006), writing from a contemporary object relations perspective, similarly suggests a change in the goal of psychoanalysis, stating that Bion's work shifted our attention from the contents of thought, the historical or narrative dimension, to the poetic or procedural dimension, the capacity to create meaning, to symbolize, and dream. Ferro (2006, p. 990) states: "The focus is no longer on a psychoanalysis that aims to remove the veil of repression or to integrate splittings, but on a psychoanalysis interested in the development of the tools that allow the development and creation of thought, that is the mental apparatus for dreaming, feeling and thinking."

We may also think of the use of poetic metaphors as reflecting a symmetrical, presentational strategy of interpretation rather than an asymmetrical, discursive strategy that explains experience in terms of linear time and causal relationship. For example, an interpretation such as "you have difficulty with authority because you always yearned for your father's attention and did not get it," attempts to make explicit the relationship between past and present, explaining, or actually translating, current emotional and relational difficulties as repetitions of past experience. Presentational, symmetrical, metaphorical interpretations involve the language of poetry, art, literature, and dreams, evoke affective experiences, creating identifications with implicit, unconscious aspects of experience, expanding and enriching life. For example, I suggested (Newirth, 2003) that a patient might "buy a slave" as a way of addressing his unrelenting complaints and hostile fantasies about his wife, one in a repeating line of women who did not love him as he wished. Like a poem, my suggestion that he "buy a slave" reflects the complex, disowned desires, disappointments, and existential dilemmas that we all face as we search for love. Poetic language and symmetrical, presentational symbols represent experience in dramatic moments in which analyst and patient participate in an affectively intense and often transgressive experience.

Ogden (1995, 1997) has written several papers on the relationship between poetry and psychoanalysis emphasizing the importance of dream-like, poetic language in creating meaning in psychoanalysis. In one paper he (Ogden, 1999) describes his experience in a poetry class in which his professor, rather than asking students what they thought a poem meant, an asymmetrical question, created a different task, asking the students to see what they could do with the poem, creating a symmetrical link of identification with the poet. This difference between what something means and what we can do with it highlights the difference between asymmetrical, historical, and discursive interpretive strategies in psychoanalysis with symmetrical, presentational, symbolic strategies that create new meanings for both the analyst and the patient.

Gilligan (2015) developed an interesting poetic format, a poetic voice within a feminist research perspective. She developed a relational approach to understanding and presenting women's unspoken experience, allowing their voices to be expressed and heard, in which she emphasized subjective experiences of agency. She describes this method as The Listening Guide, and presents her participants' experiences as "I Poems." An "I Poem" is developed or created, by sequentially presenting a participant's "I statements" in the form of a poem, thus giving voice to a woman's experience. One of her students (Koelsch, 2015) studied agency in women who had experienced unwanted sexual assaults that had not been reported. Traditional research methods for studying unreported sexual assaults would focus on issues of correspondence: how the subjects' experience and behavior were correlated with external factors in relation to preselected categories, such as prior knowledge of the perpetrator, familial history, or impaired functioning at the time. Gilligan's (2015) feminist, qualitative approach to understanding this problem presents a form of transformational validity, which focuses on articulating and experiencing women's voices and through this symmetrical, poetic, presentational approach we become able to subjectively know, to identify with and deeply understand the participants' experience of self and agency. The following "I Poem" reflects a 19-year-old college freshman's experience of an unwanted sexual assault. She and her then-boyfriend were alone and intoxicated during the incident:

I first lost my virginity
I was drunk
I've ever had
I was like
I'm not ready for this
I was like
I was a senior
no I was a junior
like I said

I was like "no"
"I want to wait"
I-he like put it in
I don't know
I was
I might as well
I obviously

This "I Poem" is very powerful, evoking multiple experiences, not the least of which is a sense of this young woman's confusion, sadness, and self-doubt. Again, like with other presentational symbols, we cannot help but identify with this young woman's painful experience. I also imagine that as she read her "I Poem" she was able to experience her pain in a different, symbolic way, feeling more potential for agency and hopefully less shame.

CLINICAL ILLUSTRATIONS OF THE POETIC FUNCTION

Many other authors (see also Kristeva, 1984; Bass, 2014a) describe dual organizations of experience which we have described as presentational, symmetrical, metaphorical, and poetic in contrast to discursive, asymmetrical, and narrative. These dual organizations of experience represent alternative interpretive strategies. In the remainder of this chapter, I want to present my use of poetic language and the poetic function in psychoanalysis and psychoanalytic psychotherapy as part of a symmetrical approach to increase patients' ability to transform concrete experiences, signs of emotional distress, into symbolic, metaphorical organizations through which subjective meaning can be developed.

Jim is a patient I have been seeing for about one year. He began therapy at his wife's urging because he not infrequently gets drunk, blacks out, and remembers little of the experience, sometimes waking in the hallway outside their apartment, and rarely knowing how he arrived there. These periodic binges arouse a great deal of anxiety in his wife and now also in me. Although Jim behaves like a "good patient," he experiences little anxiety in connection to his drinking and blackouts. In discussing one of these recent incidents, Jim seemed unconcerned, as if he was describing a mundane event that happened to someone else. Sitting with Jim feels both distant and frustrating as I recognize that he is not concerned about his drinking and that only his wife and I experience bouts of anxious concern about his periodic drunks. Although we had connected his drinking to early experiences of being controlled by his mother and to his angry feelings toward his wife, these historic and discursive interpretations seemed to have little effect. I frequently felt deeply frustrated and discounted as an analyst, as if my efforts were pointless and that my only satisfaction was financial.

Jim is a businessman and one day as we were discussing a recent blackout, I was again thinking about how his wife and I seemed to be the only ones experiencing anxious concern for his well-being. I thought that like sending jobs overseas to third world countries, he had outsourced his anxiety and feelings about drinking to his wife and me. For the first time in a while my mind felt alive; in my reverie I imagined myself as a low paid worker in a factory in Asia, totally disconnected from the efforts I made. I imagined myself as a worker doing menial repetitive tasks, in a psychic factory dealing with these outsourced emotions. I decided to tell Jim my reverie, using this poetic metaphor, I described myself as a worker in a third world country that Jim had outsourced his anxiety to, Jim responded with unusual enthusiasm and a sense of recognition and said: "I outsource most of my feeling." This was the first time that I felt we were meeting in an emotional, transitional space of mutuality and understanding where we could begin to create symbolic meaning in his previously deadened emotional world. As it often happens in a moment like this, it is hard to describe where this metaphor came from: was it mine, was it Jim's, or did I finally understand Jim's experiential world and not impose the maternal anxieties of his having to be a good boy, which was his usual self presentation, which he both loved and hated?

I have been working with Anna for a long time. She had made a great deal of progress in our work which was interrupted several years ago when she was suddenly diagnosed and treated for stage four breast cancer. She has had innumerable experiences of horror since her diagnosis, including multiple surgeries, which at times resulted in infections that required additional hospitalizations and further treatment. She had radiation, chemotherapy, implants that eventually needed to be removed, and more infections. Although Anna had a great deal of strength, her obsessional, asymmetrical approach to life complicated her experience of "living in the land of the sick" as she would say ironically. She always needed to be a good, cooperative patient as she had been a good and cooperative daughter.

Her life and our sessions were filled with the despair of her next medical visit and what I began to feel was a job-like existence, in which I wondered why she did not curse her fate and give up. I doubted that I could have survived the stress that her life presented and felt shameful and inadequate for my lack of empathy and compassion. She was going to see a new oncologist and began the session talking, in a despairing empty voice, describing her efforts staying up the previous night in order to gather her medical records together in a single binder which included the chronology of her treatments, tests, and medical data which she has accumulated since being diagnosed with cancer. Both of us were feeling overwhelmed and had difficulty finding words other than talking very concretely about her experience of this illness, of meeting with one more doctor, and of being trapped in the world of cancer.

I was surprised at what happened next. Spontaneously and loudly I said, Oy! Anna responded by saying in the same exaggerated tone that I had used, Oy! We continued, rhythmically saying Oy! As I reflected on this session, I believe we created an Oy! Poem, that I would like to present. I think that this Oy! Poem gave voice to each of our experiences and created an opportunity to break through the bonds of despair, the Lacanian Real, her illness, and to feel a sense of agency, of having fate in our hands, of paradoxically expressing our hopelessness within a hopeful, transitional experience, a poem. I want to present our Oy! Poem in written form.

> Oy!
> Oy!
> Oy!
> Oy!
> Oy!
> Oy!
> Oy!
> Oy!
> Looking at the Binder with her Medical records
> I said
> You are the best student
> dotting every "i" and crossing every "t"
> she proudly acknowledged her competence and compliance
> I am sure that you will get a prize
> the Golden Globe
> Do you have your acceptance speech?
> I am not going to thank anyone!
> I am going to thank me
> and say
> Fuck You to Everyone!

I think that we were both surprised at her emerging anger, her rarely expressed wish to say: "Fuck You to Everyone"! This Oy! Poem, opened up both of our deadened, extremely asymmetrical experiences of being a passive object as a patient with cancer. This poetic enactment allowed us to express deeply held feelings of hopelessness and rage, and move into a more alive, symmetrical symbolic relationship.

Several months later as my patient and I became stuck again in the external world of asymmetrical experiences, largely focused on tasks in the external world. It felt as if we were both going through the motions of therapy with little subjective meaning being developed. I felt like a fraud, that I was failing as her therapist, and we sunk into parallel feelings of despair. As I listened to my patient's unending sense of feeling persecuted and unhappy, I began to think of how she seemed unable to organize her experience, to differentiate important experiences from trivial experiences, leading her to feel flooded and overwhelmed by the concreteness of life. I began thinking that this is all shit and felt that we were drowning in a pool of the horrors of life. I felt embarrassed thinking about my patient's real problems as shit; however, my reverie seemed to provide me with the mental space to begin a process of reverie, of self-reflection, affectively elaborating my thoughts. I remembered long ago, on my internship, I learned that Fritz Perls, the founder of Gestalt therapy, would differentiate chicken shit from bull shit and finally elephant shit. I began imagining giving my patient a homework assignment of classifying her experiences during the day in terms of these three types of shit. I thought that this was a fairly crazy idea and laughed to myself thinking of this as a "CBT homework assignment," as if I had become a "traitor" to psychoanalysis. However, as my reverie continued I did suggest this homework assignment, that my patient keep a calendar in which she assigns a shit designation to each of her daily activities. She was at first reluctant but as a good teacher I insisted that she do her homework. She did her assignment over the next several weeks which allowed her to experience greater subjective control and to begin generating a greater sense of subjective meaning. This "homework assignment" illustrates a symmetrical, metaphoric enactment that can also be thought of as part of an implicit procedural system of learning. Like many clinical interventions that are reported it seemed effective; it enlivened and expanded our experience both in and outside of therapy. I also want to emphasize the structural elements of this interpretation that I hope would allow others to develop the courage to try something outside of the usual asymmetrical strategies.

These case vignettes illustrate how the poetic, symmetrical, presentational process transforms disconnected, dissociated language and symptoms through the mutual creation of poetic and metaphorical experiences. This poetic process occurs as patient and analyst progressively symbolize the concrete, repetitive, disturbing moments of a patient's life, along with the complex transference countertransference enactments, which like a series of squiggles (Winnicott, 1971b), generate deep affective meaning. The poetic function elaborates Winnicott's concept of transitional experience, and the Kleinian concept of symbolization, shifting the analyst's awareness and language from discursive, asymmetrical thought and language to presentational, symmetrical, evocative language, thought, and imagery. Clinically, the poetic function involves developing a theatrical space, a stage, on which both analyst and patient can play, be absurd, tell jokes, sing songs, and truly free associate.

CONCLUSION AND FUTURE DIRECTIONS

These clinical illustrations highlight the difference between asymmetrical and symmetrical interpretive strategies. These different approaches reflect an evolving understanding of how the mind organizes information and generates meaning within the parallel mental structures described in neuropsyhology, cognitive psychology, developmental psychology, and psychoanalysis. Both in the practice of psychotherapy and in research on the effectiveness of psychotherapy the distinction between symmetrical and asymmetrical strategies are rarely taken into account as we focus on the patient's psychopathology and treatment outcome, minimally studying the therapist's contribution. This book has largely focused on the therapist's contribution to the work of psychotherapy and the supervision of psychotherapy and attempted to focus on the different organizations of the therapist's contribution to the process. It would be extremely important in the future to expand our understanding of these right brain, implicit, procedural, and symmetrical processes in the transformation of the concrete signs and experiences of distress that patients and therapists experience into more symbolic, symmetrical, dream-like metaphors which create new meanings and facilitate our movement into the future.

NOTES

1. Freud's adopting the story of Oedipus became a powerful metaphor for interpreting the difficulty we have in accepting the tragic elements of our life and that fate is something beyond our individual grandiose wishes.

2. Psychoanalysis was thought of as a positivist, scientific discipline which was based on the Cartesian separation of mind and body.

References

Ammaniti, M., & Trentini, C. (2009). How new knowledge about parenting reveals the neurobiological implications of intersubjectivity: a conceptual synthesis of recent research. *Psychoanalytic Dialogues*, *19*, 537–555.

Arango, A. (2014). *Metaphor and Fields: Common Ground, Common Language, and the Future of Psychoanalysis* edited by S. Montana Katz Routledge, New York and London, 2013; *Int. J. Psycho-Anal.*, *95* (6):1321-1326.

Arlow, J. A. (1987). The Dynamics of Interpretation. *Psychoanal. Q.*, *56*, 68–87.

Arnsten, A. F. T. (1998). The biology of being frazzled. *Science*, *280*, 1711–1712.

Aron, L. (1990). One-person and two-person psychologies and the method of psychoanalysis. *Psychoanal. Psychol.*, *7*, 475–435.

Aron, L. (1992a). From Ferenczi to Searles and Contemporary Relational Approaches. Commentary on Mark Blechner's "Working in the Countertransference." *Psychoanal. Dial.*, *2*(2), 181–190.

Aron, L. (1992b). Interpretation as Expression of the Analyst's Subjectivity.*Psychoanal. Dial.*, *2*(4), 475–507.

Asari, T., Konishi, S., Jimura, K., Chikazoe, J., Nakamura, N., & Miyashita, Y. (2008). Right temporopolar activation associated with unique perception. *NeuroImage*, *41*, 145–152.

Bader, M. J. (1994), The analyst's use of humor. In H. Strean (Ed.) *The Use of Humor in Psychotherapy*. Northvale, NJ: Aronson.

Baker, R. (1993). Some reflections on humor in psychoanalysis. *Internat. J. Psycho-Anal.*, 951–960.

Bartels, A., & Zeki, S. (2000). The neural basis of romantic love. *Neuroreport*, *11*(17), 3829–3834.

Bartels, A., & Zeki, S. (2004). The neural correlates of maternal and romantic love. *Neuroimage*, *21*(3), 1155–1166.

Bass, A. (2014a). Three pleas for a measure of uncertainty, reverie, and private contemplation in the chaotic, interactive, nonlinear dynamic field of interpersonal/intersubjective relational psychoanalysis. *Psychoanalytic Dialogues*, *24*, 663–675.

Bass, A. (2014b). Supervision and Analysis at a Crossroad: The Development of the Analytic Therapist: Discussion of Papers by Joan Sarnat and Emanuel Berman. *Psychoanalytic Dialogues*, *24*(5), 540–548.

Bateson, G., Jackson, D. D., Haley, J., & Weakland, J. H. (1968). A note on the double bind (1962). In D. D. Jackson (Ed.), *Communication, family and marriage* 55–62. Palo Alto, CA: Science and Behavior Books.

Baum, H. (Producer), Hakim, R. & R. (Producers), & Buñuel, L. (Director). (1967). *Belle de Jour* [Motion Picture]. France: Valoria.

Beebe, B. (2005). Mother-Infant Research Informs Mother-Infant Treatment. *Psychoanal. St. Child, 60*, 7–46.
Benjamin, J. (1991). Father and Daughter: Identification with difference: A contribution to gender heterodoxy. *Psychoanal. Dial., 1*, 277–299.
Benjamin, J. (2000). Intersubjective Distinctions: Subjects and Persons, Recognitions and Breakdowns.*Psychoanal. Dial., 10*(1), 43–55.
Benjamin, J. (2009). A Relational Psychoanalysis Perspective on the Necessity of Acknowledging Failure in order to Restore the Facilitating and Containing Features of the Intersubjective Relationship (the Shared Third). *Int. J. Psycho-Anal., 90*(3), 441–450.
Berlin, I. (1958). You Can't Get a Man With a Gun. On *Annie Get Your Gun* [record].
Berman, E. (2000). Psychoanalytic Supervision: The Intersubjective Development. *Int. J. Psycho-Anal., 81*(2), 273–290.
Berry, B., Buck, P., Mills, M., & Stipe, M. (1991). Losing My Religion [Recorded by R.E.M.]. On *Out of Time* [Various].
Bion, W. R. (1959). Attacks on Linking. *Int. J. Psycho-Anal. 40*, 308–315.
Bion, W. R. (1962). The Psycho-Analytic Study of Thinking. *Int. J. Psycho-Anal., 43*, 306–310.
Bion, W. R. (1965). *Transformations: Change from Learning to Growth*. London: Tavistock.
Bion, W. R. (1970). *Attention and Interpretation: A Scientific Approach to Insight in Psycho-Analysis and Groups.* London: Tavistock.
Birksted-Breen, D. (2009). 'Reverberation Time,' Dreaming and the Capacity to Dream. *Int. J. Psycho-Anal., 90*, 35–51.
Blass, R. B. (2010a). Affirming 'That's not psycho-analysis!' On the value of the politically incorrect act of attempting to define the limits of our field. *The International Journal of Psychoanalysis, 91*(1), 81–89.
Blass, R. B. (2010b). An introduction to "Distinguishing psychoanalysis from psychotherapy." *The International Journal of Psychoanalysis, 91*(1), 15–21.
Blass, R. B. (2011). On the immediacy of unconscious truth: Understanding Betty Joseph's "here and now" through comparison with alternative views of it outside of and within Kleinian thinking. *International Journal of Psycho-Analysis, 92*, 1137–1157.
Blatt, S. J. (2013) The patient's contribution to the therapeutic process: A Rogerian-psychodynamic perspective. *Psychoanalytic Psychology, 30,* 139–166.
Bogdan, R. J. (1997). *Interpreting Minds*. Cambridge, MA: MIT Press.
Boston Change Process Study Group (BCPSG) (2007). The Foundational Level of Psychodynamic Meaning: Implicit Process in Relation to Conflict, Defense and the Dynamic Unconscious. *Int. J. Psycho-Anal., 88*(4), 843–860.
Bowden, E. M., & Jung Beeman, M. (1998). Getting the right idea: semantic activation in the right hemisphere may help solve insight problems. *Psychological Science, 9*, 435–440.
Bowlby, J. (1969). Attachment and Loss: Volume I: Attachment. *The International Psycho-Analytical Library, 79*, 1–401. London: The Hogarth Press and the Institute of Psycho-Analysis.
Brancucci, A., Lucci, G., Mazzatenta, A., & Tommasi, L. (2009). Asymmetries of the human social brain in the visual, auditory and chemical modalities. *Philosophical Transactions of the Royal Society of London Biological Sciences, 364*, 895–914.
Brecht, B. & Weill, K. (1928). Pirate Jenny. On *The Threepenny Opera* [record].
Breuer, J. and Freud, S. (1893). On The Psychical Mechanism of Hysterical Phenomena. *The Standard Edition of the Complete Psychological Works of Sigmund Freud, Volume II* (1893–1895): Studies on Hysteria, 1–17.
Britton, R. (1995) Psychic reality and unconscious belief. *International Journal of Psychoanalysis 76*, 19–24.
Bromberg, P. (2008). Shrinking the Tsunami: Affect Regulation, Dissociation, and the Shadow of the Flood. *Contemporary Psychoanalysis, 44*, 329–350.
Buber, M. (1970). *I and thou* (W. Kaufmann, Trans.). New York, NY: Scribner.
Bucci, W. (1997). Symptoms and symbols: A multiple code theory of somatization. *Psychoanalytic Inquiry, 12*, 151–172.

Burke, W. F. (1992). Countertransference Disclosure and the Asymmetry/Mutuality Dilemma. *Psychoanal. Dial.*, *2*(2), 241–271.

Celenza, A. (2010). The Guilty Pleasure of Erotic Countertransference: Searching For Radial True. *Studies in Gender and Sexuality, 11*(4), 175–183.

Cerqueira, J. J., Almeida, O. F. X., & Sousa, N. (2008). The stressed prefrontal cortex. Left? Right! *Brain, Behavior, and Immunity, 22*, 630–638.

Civitarese, G. & Ferro, A. (2013). The Meaning and Use of Metaphor in Analytic Field Theory. *Psychoanal. Inq., 33*(3), 190–209.

Cortina, M. and Liotti, G. (2007). New Approaches to Understanding Unconscious Processes: Implicit and Explicit Memory Systems. *Int. Forum Psychoanal., 16*(4), 204–212

Csibra, G. and Gergely, G. (1998). The teleological origins of mentalistic action explanations: A developmental hypothesis. *Devel Sci.* 1, 255–9.

Damasio, A. (1999). *The feeling of what happens. Body and emotion in the making of consciousness*. New York: Harcourt Braces.

Darcy, M. (2010). Spicy Inside-Out Roll: Dealing with Revulsion in the Analytic Space. Paper presented at the spring meeting of Division 39, Chicago, IL.

Davies, J. M. (1998). Between the Disclosure and Foreclosure of Erotic Transference-Countertransference Can Psychoanalysis Find a Place for Adult Sexuality? *Psychoanalytic Dialogues, 8*(6), 747–766.

Davies, J. M. (2003). Falling in Love with Love Oedipal and Postoedipal Manifestations of Idealization, Mourning, and Erotic Masochism. *Psychoanalytic Dialogues, 13*(1), 1–27.

Davies, J. M. & Frawley, M.G. (1992). Dissociative Processes and Transference-Countertransference Paradigms in the Psychoanalytically Oriented Treatment of Adult Survivors of Childhood Sexual Abuse. *Psychoanal. Dial., 2*(1), 5–36.

Dennett, D. (1987). *The Intentional Stance*. Cambridge, MA: MIT Press.

Dor, J. (1998) *Introduction to the Reading of Lacan: The Unconscious Structured Like a Language*. Other Press, New York.

Dylan, B. (1979). Gotta Serve Somebody [Recorded by Bob Dylan]. On *Slow Train Coming* [LP]. Sheffield, Alabama: Muscle Shoals Sound Studios.

Farber, L. H. (1999) *Lying on the Couch*. Salmagundi.

Ferenczi, S. (1931). Child-analysis in the analysis of adults. *International Journal of Psycho-Analysis,* 12, 468–482.

Ferro, A. (2006). Clinical Implications of Bion's Thought. *Int. J. Psycho-Anal., 87*(4), 989–1003.

Ferro, A. (2008). The patient as the analyst's best colleague: Transformation into a dream and narrative transformations. *Italian Psychoanalytic Annual*, 2, 199–205.

Ferro, A. (2009). Transformations in Dreaming and Characters in the Psychoanalytic Field. *Int. J. Psycho-Anal., 90*(2), 209–230.

Fonagy, P. (2000). Attachment and Borderline Personality Disorder.*J. Amer. Psychoanal. Assn.*, 48(4), 1129–1146.

Fonagy, P. (2008). A Genuinely Developmental Theory of Sexual Enjoyment and its Implications for Psychoanalytic Technique. *J. Amer. Psychoanal. Assn., 56*, 11–36 field.

Fonagy, P. & Target, M. (1996). Playing With Reality: I. Theory Of Mind And The Normal Development Of Psychic Reality. *Int. J. Psycho-Anal.*, 77, 217–233.

Fonagy, P. & Target, M. (2000). Playing with reality III: The persistence of dual psychic reality in borderline patients. *International Journal of Psycho-Analysis*, 81, 853–873.

Fonagy, P. & Target, M. (2007). Playing with Reality: IV. A Theory of External Reality Rooted in Intersubjectivity. *Int. J. Psycho-Anal., 88*(4), 917–937

Fonagy, P., Target, M., Gergely, G., Allen, J.G. and Bateman, A.W. (2003). The Developmental Roots of Borderline Personality Disorder in Early Attachment Relationships. *Psychoanal. Inq., 23*(3), 412–459.

Freud, S. (1900). The Interpretation of Dreams. *The Standard Edition of the Complete Psychological Works of Sigmund Freud,* Volume IV (1900): The Interpretation of Dreams (First Part), ix–627.

Freud, S. (1905). Jokes and their Relation to the Unconscious. *The Standard Edition of the Complete Psychological Works of Sigmund Freud, Volume VIII* (1905): Jokes and their Relation to the Unconscious, 1–247.

Freud, S. (1909). Letter from Sigmund Freud to C. G. Jung, June 18, 1909. In W. McGuire (Ed.). *The Freud/Jung Letters: The Correspondence between Sigmund Freud and C. G. Jung* (Bollingen Series, No. 94). Princeton, NJ: Princeton University Press.

Freud, S. (1910). 'Wild' Psycho-Analysis. *The Standard Edition of the Complete Psychological Works of Sigmund Freud, Volume XI* (1910): Five Lectures on Psycho-Analysis, Leonardo da Vinci and Other Works, 219–228.

Freud, S. (1920). Beyond the Pleasure Principle. *The Standard Edition of the Complete Psychological Works of Sigmund Freud, Volume XVIII* (1920–1922): Beyond the Pleasure Principle, Group Psychology and Other Works, 1–64.

Freud, S. (1923). The Ego and the Id. *The Standard Edition of the Complete Psychological Works of Sigmund Freud, Volume XIX* (1923–1925): The Ego and the Id and Other Works, 1–66.

Freud, S. (1925). A Note Upon the 'Mystic Writing-Pad.' *The Standard Edition of the Complete Psychological Works of Sigmund Freud, Volume XIX* (1923–1925): The Ego and the Id and Other Works, 225–232.

Freud, S. (1927). Humour. *The Standard Edition of the Complete Psychological Works of Sigmund Freud, Volume XXI* (1927–1931): The Future of an Illusion, Civilization and its Discontents, and Other Works, 159–166. […]

Freud, S. (1930). Civilization and its Discontents. *The Standard Edition of the Complete Psychological Works of Sigmund Freud, Volume XXI* (1927–1931): The Future of an Illusion, Civilization and its Discontents, and Other Works, 57–146.

Freud, S. (1937). Constructions in Analysis. *The Standard Edition of the Complete Psychological Works of Sigmund Freud, Volume XXIII* (1937–1939): Moses and Monotheism, An Outline of Psycho-Analysis and Other Works, 255–270

Freud, S. (1950). Project for a Scientific Psychology (1950 [1895]). *The Standard Edition of the Complete Psychological Works of Sigmund Freud, Volume I* (1886–1899): Pre-Psycho-Analytic Publications and Unpublished Drafts, 281–391. […]

Fromm, E. (1970). *The Crisis of Psychoanalysis*. New York: Holt Rhinehart and Winston.

Fromm-Reichmann, F. (2015). *Principles of intensive psychotherapy*. University of Chicago Press.

Gabbard, G. O. (1997). A Reconsideration Of Objectivity In The Analyst. *Int. J. Psycho-Anal.*, 78, 15–26.

Gabbard, G. O., & Westen, D. (2003). Rethinking therapeutic action. *Revista de Psiquiatria do Rio Grande do Sul, 25*(2), 257–273.

Gergely, G., Csibra, G. (1996). *Understanding rational actions in infancy: Teleological interpretations without mental attribution. Symposium on ' Early Perception of Social Contingencies . '* Paper presented at: the 10th Biennial International Conference on Infant Studies, Providence, RI, USA, 18–21 April.

Gergely, G., Csibra, G. (1997). Teleological reasoning in infancy: The infant's naive theory of rational action. A reply to Premack and Premack. *Cognition,* 63, 227–33.

Gergely, G., Csibra, G. (2003). Teleological reasoning in infancy: The naive theory of rational action. *Trends Cogn Sci* 7, 287–92.

Gershwin, G. (Composer), Gershwin, I. & Heyward, D. (Lyriciscts). (1935). Porgy and Bess [Score and parts]. Boston, MA.

Gershwin, G. (1934a). I Got Plenty o' Nuttin.' On *Porgy and Bess* [record].

Gershwin, G. (1934b). Summertime. On *Porgy and Bess* [record].

Gerson, S. (1996). Neutrality, Resistance, and Self-Disclosure in an Intersubjective Psychoanalysis. *Psychoanal. Dial.*, *6*(5), 623–645.

Gilligan, C. (2015). Introduction: The listening guide method of psychological inquiry. *Qualitative Psychology, 2*(1), 69–77.

Ginot, E. (2009). The Empathic Power of Enactments. *Psychoanal. Psychol.*, 26, 290–309.

Graziano, M. S., & Gross, C. G. (1994). Mapping space with neurons. *Current Directions in Psychological Science, 3*(5), 164–167.

Green, A. (1995). Has Sexuality Anything To Do With Psychoanalysis? *International Journal of Psychoanalysis, 76*(5), 871–883.
Greer, G. (1970). *The Female Eunuch*. Paladin.
Grosskyrth, P. (1986) *Melanie Klein. Her World and Her Work.* Cambridge, MA: Harvard University *Press*
Grotstein, J. S, (1995), Orphans of the "real": Some modern and postmodern perspectives on the neurobiological and psychosocial dimensions of psychosis and other primitive emotional states. *Bull. Menn. Clin.*, 59, 287–332.
Grotstein, J. S. (1979). Who is the Dreamer who Dreams the Dream and who is the Dreamer who Understands It—A Psychoanalytic Inquiry Into the Ultimate Nature of Being. *Contemp. Psychoanal.,* 15, 110–169.
Grotstein, J. S. (2000). *Who is the Dreamer Who Dreams the Dream? A Study of Psychic Presences.* New York: Relational Perspectives Book Series.
Grotstein, J. S. (2007). *A Beam of Intense Darkness: Wilfred Bion's Legacy to Psychoanalysis.* London: Karnac.
Guntrip, H. (1975). My Experience of Analysis with Fairbairn and Winnicott—(How Complete a Result Does Psycho-Analytic Therapy Achieve?). *Int. R. Psycho-Anal.*, 2, 145–156.
Hamilton, V. (1993). *Narcissus and Oedipus: the children of psychoanalysis*. Karnac Books.
Hanly, C. (1990). The Concept of Truth in Psychoanalysis. *Int. J. Psycho-Anal.,* 71, 375–383
Hoffman, I. Z. (2014). *Ritual and spontaneity in the psychoanalytic process: A dialectical-constructivist view*. Routledge.
Hughes, L. (1995). *The collected poems of Langston Hughes*. New York: First Vintage Classic Editions.
Joseph, B. (1985). Transference: The Total Situation. *Int. J. Psycho-Anal.*, 66, 447–454.
Jung, E. (1981). The Psychotherapy of the Psychoses in Analytic Training. *J. Anal. Psychol.*, *26*(4), 313–327
Khan, M. M. (1973). The Role of Illusion in the Analytic Space and Process. *Ann. Psychoanal., 1*, 231–246.
Khan, M. R. (1975). Freud and the Crises of Responsibility in Modern Psychotherapeutics. *Int. R. Psycho-Anal., 2*, 25–41
Klein, M. (1946) Notes on Some Schizoid Mechanisms. *Int. J. Psycho-Anal.* 27, 99–110.
Klein, M. (1975a) *Love, Guilt and Reperation and Other Works 1921–1945.* Delacorte Prss/ Seymour Lawrence, New York.
Klein, M. (1975b) *Envy and Gratitude and Other Works 1946–1963.* Delacorte Prss/Seymour Lawrence, New York.
Koelsch, L. E. (2015) I poems: Evoking self. *Qualitative Psychology, 2*(1), 96–107.
Kohut, H. (1984). *How Does Analysis Cure*. The University of Chicago Press, Chicago.
Kounios, J. & Beeman, M. The Aha! Moment: The cognitive neuroscience of insight. *Current Directions in Psychological Science, 18*, (4), 210–216.
Kristeva, J. (1984) *Revolution in poetic language*. New York, NY: Columbia University Press.
Lacan, J. (1981) *The Seminar of Jacques Lacan: The Four Fundamental Concepts of Psychoanalysis* (Book XI). New York, NY: Norton Publishers.
Lacan, J. (1996) *Ecrits.* New York, Norton
Lacan, J. (2007). *Seminar XVII: The other side of psychoanalysis* (Trans. R. Griggs). New York and London: Norton.
Lacan, J. (1998). *The Four Fundamental Concepts of Psycho-analysis.* New York: W. W. Norton & Company.
Lakoff, G. & Johnson, M. (1999) Philosophy in the Flesh: the Embodied Mind & its Challenge to Western Thought . New York, Basic Books
Langer, S. (1942) *Philosophy in a New Key*. Cambridge, MA: Harvard University Press.
Levenson, E. A. (1972). *The fallacy of understanding*. New York, Basic Books
Lichtenberg, J. Lachmann, F. & Fosshage, J. (1992), *Self and Motivational Systems*. Hillsdale, NJ: The Analytic Press.
Lichentenberg, J. D., Lachman, F. M., Fosshage, J. L., & Rotenberg, C. T. (1997). The Clinical Exchange: Techniques Derived from Self and Motivational Systems. *Journal of the American Academy of Psychoanalysis, 25*(4), 714–715.

Main, M., Tomasini, & L., Tolan, W. (1979). Differences among mothers of infants judged to differ in security of attachment. *Devel. Psychol.* 15, 472–3.

Malatesta, C. Z., Culver, C., Tesman, J. R., Shepard, B. (1989). The development of emotion expression during the first two years of life. *Monograph of the Society for Research in Child Dev* 54, 219.

Mancia, M. (2006). Implicit Memory and Early Unrepressed Unconscious. *Int. J. Psycho-Anal.*, *87*(1), 83–103.

Mancia, M. (2008). The Early Unrepressed Unconscious in Relation to Matte-Blanco's Thought.*Int. Forum Psychoanal.*, 17(4), 201–212.

Mashal, N., Faust, M., Hendler, T., & Jung-Beeman, M. (2007). An fMRI investigation of the neural correlates underlying the processing of novel metaphoric expressions. *Brain and Language*, *100*, 115–126.

Matte-Blanco, I. (1975) *The Unconscious as Infinite Sets.* London, Karnack Books.

Matte-Blanco, I. (1988). *Thinking, Feeling and Being: Clinical Reflections on the Fundamental Antinomy of Human Beings and the World.* London: New Library of Psychoanalysis.

Milner, M. (1993). The role of illusion in symbol formation. *Transitional objects and potential spaces: Literary uses of DW Winnicott*, 13–39.

Milton, J. (2007). *Paradise lost*. Pearson Education.

Mitchell, S. A. (1991). Contemporary Perspectives on Self: Toward an Integration. *Psycho-anal. Dial.*, 1(2), 121–147.

Mitchell, S. A. (1997). Psychoanalysis and the degradation of romance. *Psychoanalytic Dialogues*, *7*(1), 23–41.

Mitchell, S. A. (1998) The Analyst's Knowledge and Authority. *Psychoanal Q*., 67, 1–31.

Nahum, J. P. (2008). Forms of Relational Meaning: Issues in the Relations Between the Implicit and Reflective-Verbal Domains.*Psychoanal. Dial.*, *18*(2), 125–148.

Naito, E., Roland, P. E., Grefkes, C., Choi, H. J., Eickhoff, S., Geyer, S., et al. (2005). Dominance of the right hemisphere and role of Area 2 in human kinesthesia. *Journal of Neurophysiology*, *93*, 1020–1034.

Narvaez, D. (2010). Moral complexity: The fatal attraction of truthiness and the importance of mature moral functioning. *Perspectives in Psychological Science*, *5*, 163–181.

Newirth, J. (2003) *Between Cognition and Emotion: The Generative Unconscious*. New York, NY: Other Press.

Newirth, J. (2010). The Broken Container and the Analyst's Intolerable Affects. Paper presented at the spring meeting of Division 39, Chicago, IL.

Newirth, J. (2014). The Psychoanalytic Vision: The Experiencing Subject, Transcendence, and the Therapeutic Process. *Contemp. Psychoanal.*, *50*(1–2), 281–284.

Newirth, J. (2016). Frankenstein, Spellbound, and World War Z: Evolving Concepts of the Unconscious. *Psychoanalytic Psychology*, *33*S(Supplement):S75–S89

Oelsner, R., & Oelsner, M. (2005). About Supervision: An Interview with Donald Meltzer. *British Journal of Psychotherapy*, *21*, 455–461.

Ogden, T. H. (1979). On Projective Identification. *Int. J. Psycho-Anal.*, *60*, 357–373.

Ogden, T. H. (1989). On the Concept of an Autistic-Contiguous Position. Int. J. Psycho-Anal., 70, 127–140.

Ogden, T. H. (1992). The dialectically constituted/decentered subject of psychoanalysis. II: The contributions of Klein and Winnicott. *International Journal of Psycho-analysis*, 75, 3–20.

Ogden, T. H. (1994), The analytic third: Working with intersubjective clinical facts. *Internat. J. Psychoanal.*, 75, 3–20.

Ogden, T. H. (1995). Analysing Forms Of Aliveness And Deadness Of The Transference-Countertransference. *Int. J. Psycho-Anal.*, 76, 695–709.

Ogden, T. H. (1997). Reverie and interpretation. *Psychoanalytic Quarterly*, *66*, 567–595

Ogden, T. H. (1999). 'The Music of What Happens' in Poetry and Psychoanalysis. *Int. J. Psycho-Anal.*, *80*(5), 979–994.

Ogden, T. H. (2003). On not being able to dream. *Int. J. Psycho-Anal.*, 84, 17–30.

Ogden, T. H. (2004a). On holding and containing, being and dreaming. *Int. J. Psycho-Anal.*, 85, 1349–1364.

Ogden, T. H. (2004b). The Art of Psychoanalysis: Dreaming Undreamt Dreams and Interrupted Cries. *International Journal of Psychoanalysis, 85,* 857–878.

Ogden, T. H. (2005). On psychoanalytic supervision. *Int. J. Psycho-Anal., 86*(5), 1265–1280.

Ogden, T. H. (2007). On talking-as-dreaming. *Int. J. Psycho-Anal.*, 88, 575–589.

Ogden, T. H. (2010). On Three Forms of Thinking: Magical Thinking, Dream Thinking, and Transformative Thinking. *Psychoanal. Q.*, *79*(2), 317–347.

Pasquali, G. (1986), Some notes on humor in psychoanalysis. *Internat. J. Psycho-Anal.,* 14, 231–236.

Piaget, J. (1973). The Affective Unconscious and the Cognitive Unconscious. *J. Amer. Psychoanal. Assn.,* 21, 249–261.

Poland, W. (1990). The gift of laughter: On the development of a sense of humor in psychoanalysis. *Psychoanal. Quar.*, 54, 197–225.

Porter, C. (1934). Miss Otis Regrets. On *Hi Diddle Diddle* [record].

Rayner, E. (1995). *Unconscious Logic: An Introduction to Matte Blanco's Bi-Logic and Its Uses*. London: Routledge,

Raz, A. (2004). Anatomy of attentional networks. *Anatomical Records, 281B*, 21–36.

Reale, K. (2010). Trying to Clean Up the Mess: Chaos and Control in the Analytic Space. Paper presented at the spring meeting of Division 39, Chicago, IL.

Reik, T. (1948). *Listening with the Third Ear: The Inner Experience of a Psychoanalyst.* New York: Farrar, Straus and Giroux.

Renik, O. (1995). The Role Of An Analyst's Expectations In Clinical Technique: Reflections On The Concept Of Resistance. *J. Amer. Psychoanal. Assn.*, 43, 83–94.

Riolo, F. (2007). Psychoanalytic Transformations. *Int. J. Psycho-Anal., 88*(6), 1375–1389.

Rizzolatti, G. & Arbib, M. (1998), Language within our grasp. *Trends Neurosci.*, 21, 188–194.

Rodgers, R. & Hammerstein, O. (1958). I Enjoy Being a Girl. On *Flower Drum Song* [record].

Rosenblatt, A. D., & Thickstun, J. T. (1994). Intuition and consciousness. *The Psychoanalytic Quarterly, 63*(4), 696–714.

Sandkuhler, S., & Bhattacharya, J. (2008). Deconstructing insight: EEG correlates of insightful problem solving. *PLoS ONE, 1*, e1459.

Sarnat, J. (2014). Disruption and Working Through in the Supervisory Process: A Vignette From Supervision of a Psychoanalytic Candidate. *Psychoanal. Dial., 24*(5), 532–539.

Sartre, J. P., & Camus, A. (2015). *No exit and three other plays*. Vintage.

Schafer, R. (1976). *A new language for psychoanalysis*. New Haven, CT: Yale University Press.

Schimel, J. L. (1978). The Function of Wit and Humor in Psychoanalysis. *Journal of the American Academy of Psychoanalysis: Vol. 6*, No. 3, pp. 369-379.

Schlesinger, K. (1979), Jewish humor as Jewish identity. *Internat. Rev. Psycho-Anal.,* 6, 317–330.

Schooler, J. W., & Melcher, J. (1995). The ineffability of insight. In S. M. Smith, T. B. Ward, R. A. Finke (Eds.), *The creative cognition approach* (pp. 97–133). Cambridge, MA, US: The MIT Press.

Schore, A. N. (1994). *Affect regulation and the origin of the self.* Mahwah, NJ: Erlbaum.

Schore, A. N. (2000). Attachment and the regulation of the right brain. *Attachment and Human Development, 2*, 23–47.

Schore, A. N. (2003a). *Affect dysregulation and disorders of the self.* New York: Norton.

Schore, A. N. (2003b) *Affect Regulation and the Repair of the Self.* Norton. New York.

Schore, A. N. (2007). Review of *Awakening the Dreamer: Clinical Journeys* by Philip M. Bromberg. *Psychoanalytic Dialogues, 17*, 753–767.

Schore, A. N. (2009a). Attachment trauma and the developing right brain: Origins of pathological dissociation. In P. F. Dell & J. A. O'Neil (Eds.), *Dissociation and the dissociative disorders: DSM – V and beyond* (pp. 107–141). New York: Routledge.

Schore, A. N. (2009b). Relational trauma and the developing right brain: an interface of psychoanalytic self psychology and neuroscience. *Annals of the New York Academy of Sciences, 1159*, 189–203.

Schore, A. N. (2011). The right brain implicit self lies at the core of psychoanalysis. *Psychoanalytic Dialogues,21*(1), 75–100.

Searles, H. (1979) *Countertransference and Related Subjects*. New York, International Universities Press.

Segal, H. (1950). Some Aspects of the Analysis of a Schizophrenic. *Int. J. Psycho-Anal.*, 31, 268–278.

Segal, H. (1978). On Symbolism. *Int. J. Psycho-Anal.*, 59, 315–319.

Segal, H. (1994). Salman Rushdie and the Sea of Stories: A Not-So-Simple Fable about Creativity. Int. J. Psycho-Anal., 75, 611–618.

Shoenhals, H. (1996). Triangular space and symbolization. *Psychoanalytic Inquiry*, 16, 167–183.

Siegel, D. J. (1999). *The developing mind.* New York: Guilford.

Solms, M. (2003) The Brain and the Inner World: An Introduction to the Neuroscience of Subjective Experience. Other Press, New York

Sondheim, S. (1957). I Feel Pretty. On *Westside Story* [record].

Soni, N. (2012). *Squiggles in the Dust: An Implicit Theory of Symbolization in D.W. Winnicott's Therapeutic Consultations in Child Psychiatry*. (Doctoral Dissertation).

Spence, D. P. (1982). Narrative Truth and Historical Truth: Meaning and Interpretation in Psychoanalysis. London and New York: W.W Norton and Company.

Stern, D. N. (1985). *The Interpersonal World of the Infant: A View from Psychoanalysis and Developmental Psychology*. New York: Basic Books.

Stern, D. N. (1992). The 'Pre-Narrative Envelope': An Alternative View of 'Unconscious Phantasy' in Infancy. *Bul. Anna Freud Centre*, 15(4), 291–318.

Stern, D. N. (2004). *The present moment in psychotherapy and everyday life (norton series on interpersonal neurobiology)*. WW Norton & Company.

Stern, D.N., Sander, L.W., Nahum, J.P., Harrison, A.M., Lyons-Ruth, K., Morgan, A.C., Bruschweilerstern, N. & Tronick, E.Z. (1998). Non-Interpretive Mechanisms in Psychoanalytic Therapy: The 'Something More' Than Interpretation. *Int. J. Psycho- Anal.*, 79, 903–921.

Stolorow, R. D. (2002). Impasse, Affectivity, and Intersubjective Systems. *Psychoanal. Rev., 89*(3), 329–337.

Strean, H. (1994), *The Use of Humor in Psychotherapy. Northvale*, NJ: Aronson.

Sullivan, H. S. (1953) *The Interpersonal Theory of Psychiatry*. New York, Norton.

Summers, F. (2013) *The Psychanalytic Vision*. New York, NY: Routledge.

Symington, N. (2007). A Technique for Facilitating the Creation of Mind. *Int. J. Psycho-Anal., 88*(6), 1409–1422.

Szasz, T. (1974) *The Myth of Mental Illness: Foundations of a Theory of Personal Conduct*. HarperPerenial.

Target, M. and Fonagy, P. (1996). Playing With Reality: II. The Development Of Psychic Reality From A Theoretical Perspective. *Int. J. Psycho-Anal.*, 77, 459–479.

Tulving, E. (1972). Episodic and semantic memory. *Organization of memory,1*, 381–403.

Tustin, F. (1980). Autistic Objects. *Int. Rev. Psycho-Anal.*, 7, 27–39

Welling, H. (2005). The intuitive process: the case of psychotherapy. *Journal of Psychotherapy Integration, 15*, 19–47.

Winnicott, D. W. (1955). Metapsychological and Clinical Aspects of Regression Within the Psycho-Analytical Set-Up. *Int. J. Psycho-Anal.*, 36, 16–26.

Winnicott, D. W. (1958). *Collected Papers: Through Paediatrics to Psycho-analysis*. London: Tavistock.

Winnicott, D. W. (1960). The Theory of the Parent-Infant Relationship. *Int. J. Psycho-Anal.*, 41, 585–595

Winnicott, D. W. (1969). The use of an object. *The International Journal of Psycho-Analysis,50*, 711.

Winnicott, D. W. (1971a). *Playing and Reality*. London: Tavistock Publications.

Winnicott, D. W. (1971b). Therapeutic Consultations in Child Psychiatry. *Int. Psycho-Anal. Lib.*, 87, 1–398.

Winnicott, D. W. (1974). Fear of Breakdown. *Int. Rev. Psycho-Anal., 1*, 103–107.

Wolf, N. S., Gales, M. E., Shane, E., & Shane, M. (2001). The developmental trajectory from amodal perception to empathy and communication: The role of mirror neurons in this process. *Psychoanalytic Inquiry*, *21*(1), 94–112.

Zizek, S. (1991*) Looking Awry: An Introduction to Jacques Lacan through Popular Culture*. Boston, MIT Press.

Index

About the Author

Joseph Newirth has been a professor at the Derner Institute of Advanced Psychological Studies, Adelphi University, for over 30 years. He is on the core clinical faculty where he teaches courses in psychoanalytic theory and technique. He is the former director of the Postdoctoral Program in Psychoanalysis and Psychotherapy at Adelphi University and is on the faculty and a supervisor at the NYU Postdoctoral Program in Psychotherapy and Psychoanalysis and the National Training Program at the National Institute for the Psychotherapies. He has presented papers in Division 39 of the American Psychological Association, national and international confrerences, as well as being invited to present papers at Psychoanalytic Institutes and international conferences. His book *Between Emotion and Cognition: The Generative Unconscious* was published in 2003 by The Other Press, NY. This book received the Gradiva Prize and Honorable Mention for the Goethe Prize.

www.ingramcontent.com/pod-product-compliance
Ingram Content Group UK Ltd.
Pitfield, Milton Keynes, MK11 3LW, UK
UKHW041123071026
15587UKWH00009B/107

9 781498 576840